A Brief History of

Islam

Blackwell Brief Histories of
Religion

This series offers brief, accessible and lively accounts of key topics within theology and religion. Each volume presents both academic and general readers with a selected history of topics which have had a profound effect on religious and cultural life. The word "history" is, therefore, understood in its broadest cultural and social sense. The volumes are based on serious scholarship but they are written engagingly and in terms readily understood by general readers.

Published

Alister E. McGrath – A Brief History of Heaven
G. R. Evans – A Brief History of Heresy
Tamara Sonn – A Brief History of Islam

Forthcoming

Douglas Davies – A Brief History of Death
Lawrence Cunningham – A Brief History of Saints
Michael Banner – A Brief History of Ethics
Carter Lindberg – A Brief History of Love
Carter Lindberg – A Brief History of Christianity
Dana Robert – A Brief History of Mission
Philip Sheldrake – A Brief History of Spirituality
Kenneth Appold – A Brief History of the Reformation
Dennis D. Martin – A Brief History of Monasticism
Martha Himmelfarb – A Brief History of the Apocalypse

A Brief History of
Islam

TAMARA SONN

Blackwell
Publishing

BLACKWELL PUBLISHING
350 Main Street, Malden, MA 02148-5020, USA
9600 Garsington Road, Oxford OX4 2DQ, UK
550 Swanston Street, Carlton, Victoria 3053, Australia

First published 2004 by Blackwell Publishing Ltd

3   2005

Library of Congress Cataloging-in-Publication Data

Sonn, Tamara–
    A brief history of Islam / Tamara Sonn.
       p. cm. – (Blackwell brief histories of religion)
    Includes bibliographical references and index.
    ISBN 1-4051-0902-5 (hardcover : alk. paper) – ISBN 1-4051-0900-9 (paperback : alk. paper)
1. Islam–History. 2. Islam–Essence, genius, nature. I. Title. II. Series.
BP50.S65 2004
297'.09–dc22

2003015467

ISBN-13: 978-1-4051-0902-4 (hardcover : alk. paper) – ISBN-13: 978-1-4051-0900-0 (paperback : alk. paper)

A catalogue record for this title is available from the British Library.

Set in 10/12.5pt Meridien
by Graphicraft Limited, Hong Kong
Printed and bound in the United Kingdom
by TJ International, Padstow, Cornwall

The publisher's policy is to use permanent paper from mills that operate a sustainable forestry policy, and which has been manufactured from pulp processed using acid-free and elementary chlorine-free practices. Furthermore, the publisher ensures that the text paper and cover board used have met acceptable environmental accreditation standards.

For further information on Blackwell Publishing, visit our website:
www.blackwellpublishing.com

For John

Contents

Illustrations

Maps

Foreword

Akbar S. Ahmed

When Americans defeated Saddam Hussein and occupied Baghdad in early 2003 they confronted a society with a distinctly different way of looking at history. For Americans, history moves in a linear progression. The future beckons bright and promising. For Arabs, the history of the past still inspires and informs their present. That is why, when Americans were expecting Iraqis to talk of setting up democratic institutions, media networks, and commercial institutions influenced by the West, one of the first things the Iraqis did was to march to Karbala, the site where the grandson of the prophet of Islam was martyred in the seventh century. About two million Iraqis made the pilgrimage to one of the holiest sites in Islam particularly revered by the Shia, the majority population of Iraq. The television images of this spectacle created further questions in the minds of Americans. It appeared that the Western world and the Islamic world not only looked at history differently but were doomed to stare at each other with incomprehension.

If it was so difficult to understand history, then how was the West to understand Islam itself? After September 11, 2001 the question assumed more than academic relevance. It was no longer the stuff of academic debate but involved policy and practical matters relating to what Americans called a global "war on terror" involving different Muslims living in different societies.

Scholars talked and wrote of an ongoing clash of civilizations between the Western world and the Islamic world. Outright prejudices and plain ignorance were seeping into discussions of Islam. Few in America understood the religion. After September 11, Sikhs were killed as they were mistaken for Muslims. Yet here was a civilization with 1.3 billion people and America was involved with Muslims at different levels in different countries. Indeed America's "war on terror" was primarily against members of this very population.

As a result of the intense interest around Islam, countless instant experts emerged to write books and commentaries. Many of these linked Islam to terrorism and violence and failed to provide valid explanations of either Islamic history or society. Most of these attempted to answer the basic question being asked by Americans and echoed by President George W. Bush himself: "Why do they hate us?"

The answers to this question came thick and fast but remained incomplete. Without an understanding of history it is difficult to explain Muslim behavior and impossible to understand Muslim politics.

Professor Tamara Sonn in *A Brief History of Islam* combines the skills of the historian with the insights of the scholar of Islam. Her history therefore is not simply about the rise and fall of dynasties but a clear and coherent picture of a dynamic, complex, and global religion.

In particular, she emphasizes the great clashes of ideas that have motivated Islamic history from the earliest times. History, then, is not a random series of unconnected acts; there is a clear pattern of cause and effect as Muslims attempt to live up to a notion of an ideal society inspired by their vision of God.

Professor Sonn sets the theological stage in her opening paragraph of Chapter 1. She places Islam squarely in the Abrahamic or monotheistic tradition. That opening itself indicates her sensitivity to both her subject and her audience: although Muslims will appreciate the reference, they will not be surprised; many Western readers will be, for not many know that Islam is closely related to the Abrahamic tradition.

Indeed the last paragraph of the book, so eloquently written, once again reflects this sensitivity. In the last lines Professor Sonn quotes Surah 2, Verse 177. It is in essence the definition of a good human being in the light of Quranic advice. Once again it will reassure Muslims of how well Professor Sonn has understood their religion and will no doubt inform non-Muslims of the true nature of Islam. It will also challenge many of the stereotypes of Islam depicting it as a religion of extremism and violence.

In her first chapter Professor Sonn creates the ideal model of Islam. She points out the importance of compassion and tolerance in this model. She does not avoid the more controversial aspects of Islam in the West such as polygamy. The second chapter is called "Pursuit of Knowledge in the Service of God and Humanity: The Golden Age." This was the great age of Islamic civilization: "During the Middle Ages, Islam's unique system of religious freedom and administrative flexibility allowed for remarkable stability and growth. It also produced a period of peace and prosperity in which the sciences and arts were brought to new levels of perfection. The Islamic world from Spain to India – with its plurality of cultures, ethnicities, and religious communities – produced an unrivalled cultural efflorescence."

Chapter 3 discusses division and reorganization in Muslim society and sets the stage for Chapter 4 on colonialism and reform. There is an important discussion of ijtihad, which allows Islamic law openness and flexibility. The chapter ends with a discussion that connects the great Arab historian Ibn Khaldun, living in the fifteenth century, to Muhammad Iqbal, "the advocate of dynamic, adaptable, progressive Islam" who advocated Pakistan as a modern Muslim state, in the twentieth century.

Chapter 5 discusses and is called "Obstacles and Prospects for Islamic Reform." Towards the end there is a highly relevant discussion of the mid-twentieth-century figures Hasan al-Banna and Sayyid Qutb, the fathers of the radical Islamic movements, whose influence on men like Osama bin Laden is widely acknowledged. What emerges is an appreciation of history as an ongoing dialectic between the will of people to order society according to their comprehension of God's commands and the reality of changing times. That is why there can be no understanding of contemporary Islamic political behavior without an expert on hand to help us make sense of the history motivating and informing it.

This is a book Professor Sonn was born to write. She is the right person at the right time to write a brief history of Islam. She is presently the Kenan Professor of Humanities and Professor of Religion at the College of William and Mary. Professor Sonn's Ph.D. is from the University of Chicago where she sat at the feet of the late great Islamic scholar Fazlur Rahman. She has written well-received books on Islam but is no ivory tower scholar. Until recently she was the active President for the American Council for the Study of Islamic Societies.

In the charged atmosphere around the understanding of Islam after September 11 there is perhaps no greater service a scholar of Islam can perform than helping to explain Islam in the context of its history. Most commentators have been overwhelmed by the task. That is why Professor Tamara Sonn deserves the gratitude of all those who wish to understand the post-September 11 world in which we find ourselves. In a masterly fashion and with admirable brevity she has presented us with an indispensable guide to understanding Islam in the twenty-first century.

Professor Akbar S. Ahmed
Ibn Khaldun Chair of Islamic Studies and
Professor of International Relations
American University, Washington

Preface

A Brief History of Islam was written as an introduction to the religion of nearly one-fifth of the world's population, the dominant religion in over 50 countries, and the fastest-growing religious minority in Europe and the United States. It was written as a history because nothing helps explain the current state of affairs in any community better than a description of how those affairs developed. And perhaps no community senses a greater need for understanding today than Muslims. A glance at some of the recent titles about Islam is revealing: *Islam Under Siege*; *What Went Wrong?*; *Unholy Terror* (by Akbar Ahmed, Bernard Lewis, and John Esposito, respectively). These are books that have come out only within the past year – after the infamous events of September 11. Although the atrocities committed that day constitute a tragic aberration from Islamic values and have been condemned by Muslims worldwide, they continue to color many people's perceptions of Islam. Even before September 11, Muslims felt terribly misrepresented in Western media. As early as 1989, according to Reeva Simon's *The Middle East in Crime Fiction*, Arabs and Muslims had become the most common villains in movies and crime fiction. By the mid-1990s, discussions of an emerging "clash of civilizations" between Islam and the West were inescapable in American universities, thanks to the work of historian Samuel Huntington.

How did one of the world's major religions, a tradition that inspired some of the greatest cultural achievements in the pre-modern era, come to be associated almost exclusively with terrorism and tyranny? How did a religious tradition that shares its history, beliefs, and values with Jews and Christians become so isolated?

The answer indeed lies in a clash of civilizations, but not the one Huntington writes about. The critical clash between Christendom and the Muslim world took place over the past two to three centuries. On one side were the European powers who believed that taking control of Africa and Asia was their destiny. It was the "white man's burden," part of their "civilizing mission." On the other were the people whose land, resources, and power were usurped. For them, Europe's actions were nothing but crass imperialism, and they profoundly changed the course of Islamic history (along with the history of other parts of the colonized world).

Muslims had built the most advanced civilization in the Western world by the Middle Ages. They had preserved, consolidated, and advanced the learning of the ancients, developing the world's highest levels of mathematics, science, philosophy, arts, and technology. By the time Europe began its colonial incursions, the Muslim world was undergoing change. Reformers were calling attention to the need for reorganization and modernization. But these efforts were interrupted by Europe's economic and political expansion. The combined weight of European imperialism and domestic efforts to repel imperialism was sufficient to derail reform and modernization efforts in the Islamic world. Economic development was forestalled by Europe's desire for natural resources and raw materials, rather than the products of an industrialized economy. Political development was curtailed by Europe's desire to work through local leaders willing to advance

Europe's interests. And even religious and social reform efforts were interrupted, as clinging to tradition became a symbol of resistance to the imperialists.

The countries that make up the Muslim world today achieved their independence only within the past century and, as in the rest of the formerly colonized world, only with a great deal of struggle. Typically, polite requests for independence, petitions, and demands were ignored. As efforts to achieve independence intensified, so did the intransigence of the colonial powers. Activists and resistance leaders were viewed as criminals and treated accordingly. Arrests, deportations, and executions generally eliminated civilian leadership, resulting in the militarization of independence movements. This is not to say that all problems in the Muslim world are the fault of the West; many of the problems recognized by early reformers have nothing to do with foreign intervention and many of them remain, compounded by the results of colonialism. However, the pattern just sketched does account for the prevalence of military and non-democratic rule throughout the formerly colonized world. It also accounts for high levels of hostility toward the West.

Fortunately, however, conflict with the West is neither inherent in Islamic sources nor inevitable, as we will see in the following chapters. Tracing the development of Islam from its origins in seventh-century Arabia to the present, we will see that in fact Islam is an integral part of the monotheistic tradition. Like Judaism and Christianity, its adherents worship one God, believed to be the creator and merciful judge of all humanity. Muslims revere Abraham, Moses, and Jesus, along with other figures familiar to readers of Jewish and Christian scripture. Perhaps most importantly, Muslims value human dignity and social justice as highly as any other community on earth. Islam's troubled modern history has resulted in enormous diversity of opinion about how to address the challenges of development and modernization. In some cases, political setbacks have produced desperation, radicalization, and even mutation of Islamic values.

Nevertheless, commitment to human dignity and justice remain values shared among both the victors and victims of the colonial clash. Those values constitute a common ground, a basis for communication concerning shared goals and cooperation to achieve them. Facilitating that communication and cooperation is the goal of this work.

I would like to thank my colleagues – especially John Esposito, John Voll, and Akbar Ahmed, for their insightful critiques of my work, and my students at the College of William & Mary for inspiring me to finish it. As always, my deepest appreciation goes to John and Jordan.

TS
Williamsburg, 2003

Chapter 1

Many Paths to One God: Establishing the Ideals

When Jews speak of their religion, they call it Judaism or the Judaic tradition. When Christians speak of their religious traditions, they often refer to Judeo-Christianity, since Christianity was an organic outgrowth of Judaism. In the same way, Muslims refer to their religion as part of the Abrahamic or monotheistic tradition, since Islam shares the history, basic beliefs, and values of Judaism and Christianity. Muslims consider Jews and Christians to be their siblings within the *ahl al-kitab*, the "people of the Book." This is the family of monotheists, those who believe in one supreme God (Allah, the Arabic word for God), the creator, the sustainer, the benevolent and merciful judge of all humanity. "The Book" is revelation contained in scripture; Muslims believe all revelation came from the only God, who revealed His will to humanity repeatedly, in various times and places to different groups.

The Quran (Koran, in archaic spelling) is Islamic scripture, the book containing Islamic revelation. It reiterates, confirms, and completes Jewish and Christian scriptures, referring often to the Jewish Torah and the Christian Gospels. The Quran calls all people to remember and respect the truths carried in those earlier books. Muslims believe the Quran also corrects some misinterpretations of those scriptures, but overall focuses on inspiring Jews, Christians, and Muslims to work together toward their shared goal of justice and, in so doing, to achieve eternal reward: "People of the Book, come together in agreement on a word, that we worship only God . . ." (3:65)

God has sent revelation to all communities, according to the Quran. Revelation includes specific rituals and laws, so Muslims do not find it surprising that communities differ in their perceptions and practices. The Quran also says that if God had wanted all people to be the same, He would have made them that way. "For each of you we have established a law and a way. And if God had willed it, He would have made you one community. But [He has not] so that He may test you in what He has given you . . ." The differences among religions are therefore believed to be part of the divine plan. The Quran invites all people to participate with Muslims in the struggle to do the will of God. In its words, "So compete with one another in good deeds." (5:48)

Reflecting this pluralism, the Quran most often addresses itself to "believers" (*mu'minun*, or "those who believe," *alladhina amanu*) in general, rather than followers of a specific branch of religion. People are called to practice the true religion of monotheism in general (*din*). The Quran does not try to establish a new religion, but rather to inspire people to new commitment to the one true religion of monotheism. The term *islam* is used only eight times in the Quran, and is referred to as the true religion. But in the Quran the term means the act of submitting to the divine will, rather than an organized religious group separate from other monotheistic traditions. By contrast, the term *din*, meaning the true religion revealed by the one God at various times throughout human history, is used over 90 times.

The Quran is the record of what God revealed to a specific community, the Arabs of Mecca (in what is now Saudi Arabia). The word *qur'an* means "recitation"; it records what was revealed through a prophet named Muhammad in the seventh century. Muslims believe that Muhammad was only the last in the long series of people through whom the will of God was revealed to humanity. Adam is considered the first prophet, because through the story of Adam and his wife in the garden – the same story revealed to Jews and Christians – humanity began to learn that God created us with a purpose. Fulfilling that purpose requires obedience to the divine will, and disobedience will bring suffering and punishment. The first major prophet of Islam, however, was Abraham (Ibrahim). The story of Abraham is familiar to all monotheists. He was an aged shepherd in Iraq who had longed for a child for years. God chose to favor Abraham with a child, but then asked him to demonstrate his obedience by killing his beloved son. At the last minute, God spared the child, but Abraham's willingness to sacrifice his son rather than disobey the command of God sealed the agreement between God and humanity. God promises eternal reward to all who submit to the will of God; "one who submits" to the will of God is a *muslim*. Likewise, God promised punishment for willful disobedience. One of the disagreements between Muslims and Jews concerns the identity of the son Abraham was willing to sacrifice. Muslims believe that Abraham intended to sacrifice his son Ishmael (Ismail), rather than Isaac (Ishaq), and that Muslims are thus spiritual descendants of Abraham through Ishmael and his mother Hagar (Hajar). Nevertheless, Muslims agree that Abraham's willingness to sacrifice his son was of utmost importance; in thus demonstrating his commitment to the will of God he established the covenant between God and those who serve Him. Jews and Muslims are both descendants of Abraham and heirs to that covenant.

Through the second great messenger of God, Moses (Musa), the Torah was revealed. Mentioning the Torah eighteen times, the Quran reminds believers that its guidance continues to be valid. The Quran actually describes itself as "confirming the truth of the Torah that is before me" (3:50) and calls upon believers to "bring the Torah now, and recite it." (3:93) Believers are expected to be honest, charitable, care for the needy, fast, obey dietary regulations, and overall to honor God and respect His creation, just as the Torah instructed.

The last great messenger before Muhammad was Jesus (Issa). Mentioned twenty-five times in the Quran, Jesus is called the Messiah (although the meaning of that term is not made clear), the son of a virgin, and the vehicle of great signs from God. His message, the Gospel, is confirmed and described as consistent with the messages of all prophets. Speaking through Muhammad, the Quran says that God is sending the same religion (*din*) that He sent through Noah, Abraham, Moses, and Jesus, saying: "Establish [true] religion [*din*] and do not be divided about it." (42:13) But the Quran does assert that those who believe that Jesus is divine, the son of God and part of a divine trinity, are mistaken:

> O People of Scripture, do not exaggerate your religion or say anything about God but the truth. The Messiah, Jesus son of Mary, was only a messenger of God, and His word which He sent to Mary, and a spirit from Him. So believe in God and His messenger and do not say 'Three' . . . God is only one. (4:171)

Still, like the messages of the other prophets, Jesus' message is true, according to the Quran, and the Jews were mistaken to reject it. The Quran takes special care to correct those who believe that the covenant is meant only for the descendants of Abraham. The Quran says that the determining factor in God's promise is not heredity, but the deeds of each individual. When Abraham is told that God will reward his obedience by making him a leader among his people, Abraham asks about his progeny. The response: "My covenant does not include wrongdoers." (2:124) It is not the group one belongs to that determines salvation; the Quran says that it is demonstrating submission (*islam*) to the will of God through good works that brings reward. Thus, the Quran chastises both Jews and Christians for their mutual rejection. "The Jews say the Christians have nothing to stand on, and the Christians say the Jews have nothing to stand on, while they both recite the same Scripture." (2:113) It is God who will decide on all people's fate, on the Day of Judgment, when all deeds will be weighed on the scale of justice. Those who have demonstrated their true belief through good deeds "have nothing to fear, nor shall they grieve." (2:112)

Again, the continuity of the monotheistic tradition is asserted. A number of lesser prophets – a total of 18 between the time of Adam and that of Muhammad – reiterated and reconfirmed the messages of revelation. In fact, the Quran states that every nation has been sent a messenger from God. ("Every nation has its Messenger." [10:47] See also 16:36: "We sent forth among every nation a Messenger." Cf: 16:63; 35:24) But the message was always essentially the same: God rewards those who do His will and punishes those who do not.

The Life and Teachings of Muhammad, Prophet of Islam: The Quran and Sunna

Doing the will of God is not a simple task. It includes following the laws concerning prayer, charity, fasting, pilgrimage, proper diet, and cleanliness. Those rules have been clearly established in revelation and are not subject to reinterpretation. But simply following the rules is not enough to fulfill the will of God, in the Islamic perspective. The Quran warns those who pray but then "are neglectful of their prayer," those who pray but then "mistreat orphans and scarcely work toward feeding the poor." These people, says the Quran, make a mockery of their faith (107:1–7). Praying and performing other rituals, according to the Quran, are obligatory not because they please God in themselves; they are meant to keep people focused on their reason for existing in the first place, and motivated to work toward the fulfillment of God's will in all spheres of life. The Quran says, for example, that the meat that people sacrifice does not reach God; it is for the benefit of believers that rituals are performed: "Their flesh does not reach God nor their blood, but your righteousness reaches God." (22:8) Similarly, sin does not hurt God; it hurts the sinners and their communities: "Muhammad is only a messenger, like those who have passed away before him. When he dies or is killed, will you reject [his message]? Those who do so do not hurt God; God will reward the grateful." (3:144) What is important is not the ritual of prayer or sacrifice itself, but the virtuous life and good deeds it encourages:

> A kind word with forgiveness is better than almsgiving followed by injury. God is absolute and forgiving. O believers, do not make your charity worthless through insult and injury, like the person who gives of his wealth only for show but does not believe in God and the Last Day. (2:263–64)

The Quran describes itself not as a law book or code, but as guidance for humanity (*hudan li'l-nas*, 3:4, e.g.) It was revealed over a period of some twenty-two years, during which conditions changed significantly. And with the changes in circumstances often came changes in the specific directives given to the community. In the beginning of Muhammad's career as a prophet, he had only a small group of followers. They were persecuted by the wealthy rulers of Mecca, the Quraysh family, because the Quraysh felt threatened by Muhammad's call for worship of the only God and an end to social injustice. When Muhammad and his small community were driven from their homes, forced to live in separate quarters on the outskirts of town and boycotted, they were instructed by the Quran to suffer injustice with dignity. "Call them to the way of your Lord with wisdom and good arguments and reason with them [offering] a better way . . . If you punish them, do so in the same measure as you were

punished. But if you endure patiently, it is better for you."
(16:125–26)

Despite persecution, Muhammad continued to warn people of the dire consequences of ignoring God's will. He reminded people that God's will is for a just society, one that reflects the equality all people share in the eyes of their Creator. His message was popular, and he quickly attracted a significant following in Mecca and beyond. Muhammad's reputation as a wise and just arbitrator reached Yathrib (some 250 miles north of Mecca), a town that had been suffering under inter-tribal warfare for years. Delegates from Yathrib invited Muhammad to move to their town, promising to abide by his guidance in return for his settling their disputes. After some hesitation Muhammad accepted the invitation and, with his followers, moved to Yathrib in the year 622 CE. This event begins the Islamic calendar (called the Hijra calendar, to commemorate the "emigration" from Mecca to Yathrib) owing to the profound shift that it marks in the fate of the Muslim community. In Medina, the new name of Yathrib (its full name became "City of the Prophet," *madinat al-nabi*, anglicized as Medina), the Muslims became an autonomous community, able to establish the religious practice and social vision revealed by God through Prophet Muhammad. They were able to create a community guided by the Quran's view of human dignity and compassion for the weak. As their strength increased, so did the Meccans' hostility toward them. When the Meccans tried to destroy the Muslims in Medina by confiscating their properties and attacking their families back in Mecca, the Quran guided the Muslims to fight back, rather than suffer patiently:

And fight in the way of God with those who fight you, but do not be aggressors; God does not love the aggressors. And slay them wherever you find them, and expel them from where they expelled you; persecution is more grievous than slaying . . . But if they [cease hostilities], surely God is all forgiving, all compassionate. Fight them until there is no persecution and religion is God's.

Then if they [cease hostilities], there shall be no hatred except for evildoers. (2:190)

This is an example of the kind of guidance given by the Quran that is geared toward specific circumstances. In order to understand the import of such a verse, it is necessary to know the "circumstances of revelation" (*asbab al-nuzul*), as they are known in Quranic studies; it is necessary to know what historic conditions were being addressed in the verse.[1] The verses that give specific legislation, such as the requirement for prayer, charity, fasting, pilgrimage, and dietary laws, as well as prohibitions on murder, theft, usury, prostitution, gambling, and the like, are considered eternal; there are no foreseeable circumstances in which requirements for worship will be abrogated or violations of human dignity be sanctioned. However, the majority of Quranic verses are more general, presenting a consistent and coherent vision for a just society, based on divine providence and mercy, and encouraging people to struggle to establish such a society.

The major characteristics of the society envisioned by the Quran are compassion or kindness, honesty, and justice. Variations on the term "be compassionate" or "show mercy" (*rahima*) occur hundreds of times in the Quran. In fact, "compassionate" and "merciful" are the most common descriptions of God. People are told to be kind and cherish their parents (19:14; 19:32), and even to ask forgiveness from God for them if they make mistakes (60:4). Even though Mecca initially rejected the believers, persecuted and evicted them from their homes, the believers in Medina are told that they should show kindness and justice toward those Meccans who did not participate in the aggression (60:7–8).

Charity is also extremely important in the Quranic perspective. "Surely God recompenses the charitable," we are told when the story of Joseph is being recounted (12:88). People are instructed to forgive debts owed to them as an act of charity (2:280). Charity is often described as a means of making up for offenses.

The Quran maintains the Biblical ethic of retaliation, a standard means of maintaining order in societies lacking other legal enforcement institutions. But it says that forgoing retaliation as an act of charity will help make up for sins (5:45). Charity is also prescribed as a means of self-purification (9:103). All Muslims are required to give charity according to Islamic law. The term used for this kind of charity (*zakah* or *zakat*) actually means "purification." The idea is that wealth is a good thing, as long as it is used for good purposes like helping the needy and "those whose hearts are to be reconciled," and freeing slaves and debtors (9:60).

As important as charity is in the Quranic perspective, honesty, sincerity, and compassion are stressed even more: "Honorable words and forgiveness are better than charity." (2:263) Believers are constantly reminded that truthfulness and sincerity are among the most important virtues. They are part of the overall profile of a virtuous person described in the Quran. The Quran specifies that the same criteria for virtue apply to men and women:

> Indeed, for men who submit and women who submit, men who believe and women who believe, men who obey and women who obey, men who are honest and women who are honest, men who are patient and women who are patient, men who are humble and women who are humble, men who are charitable and women who are charitable, men who fast and women who fast, men who are modest and women who are modest, men who remember God often and women who do so, God has prepared forgiveness and a great reward. (33:35)

That profile of a *muslim* (or *muslima*, the feminine form), "one who submits to the will of God," is integrally linked to perhaps the defining theme of Islamic ethics: justice. The Quran says that, overall, God has called for justice (7:29, e.g.). "Oh believers, establish justice, be witnesses for God, even if the evidence goes against yourselves or your parents or relatives, and regardless of whether someone is rich or poor; under all circumstances God has priority for you." (4:135) Justice is a broad term, one that encompasses and affects every aspect of life. There is no single formula for achieving justice; it can only be achieved by establishing a standard of human dignity and then being committed to maintaining that dignity in ever-changing circumstances. Therefore, the Quran deals with multiple aspects of justice in multiple contexts, establishing norms and giving examples. Believers are told to be kind and just at all times, for example, but it pays particular attention to the concerns of the most vulnerable in society: orphans, mentioned over twenty times.

Interestingly, the Quran's permission for polygyny (multiple wives) is made in the context of concern for orphans. In a chapter entitled "Women" (chapter/*sura* 4 of the Quran), people are told to protect the rights of orphans for whom they are responsible – if necessary, by marrying them. In seventh-century Arabia, a society plagued by warfare and poverty, there were many orphans. Female orphans were particularly at risk, since this was not a society in which women had economic independence. Unless they inherited wealth, women were entirely dependent upon men. Because of the brutality of that society towards women, female infanticide was common. People killed their baby girls, fearing they would not be able to provide for them and that they would be subjected to the whims of those who had no respect for women. Out of concern for the protection of women, the Quran forbids female infanticide. It also rebukes men who are ashamed when a daughter, rather than a son, is born. On a very practical level, it requires that females be given inheritance shares (4:4–12) and that the traditional dowry required at weddings be given as a gift to the bride (4:4), rather than to the bride's parents as a "bride price." The Quran also insists that men and women both are entitled to whatever wages they earn. With regard to the orphans in Medinan society, the Quran tells men to treat them fairly, and if they are afraid that orphans are not being treated fairly, then they may protect them by marrying up to four, but only if they can treat them all impartially. If they do not feel they can avoid slighting one of their wives, then they should only marry one (4:3). Although the focus of this verse is compassion for the weak and equity for women, traditional interpreters conclude that it simply allows men to marry four wives at a time. Modern interpreters tend to return to the focus of justice and incorporate the Quran's high ideals for mutually satisfactory spousal relationships when discussing marriage. The Quran says that spouses were created by God to find comfort in one another and to be bound by "love and mercy" (30:21). As a result, many modern interpreters believe the Quran advocates monogamy except under extraordinary circumstances (i.e., like those of seventh-century Arabia). In view of the Quran's emphasis on human equality, many modern interpreters believe the Quran's goal is to establish societies in which polygyny is not necessary to protect women.

Another group for whom the Quran shows special concern are debtors. Charity is to be used to help debtors, and people are supposed to pardon debts owed to them as an act of charity. The Quran is particularly concerned with abolishing usury, which was common in seventh-century Arabia. Pre-Islamic records indicate that interest rates were exorbitant. The Quran therefore forbids usury, stating that usurers "will not rise again." (2:275) In this context of concern for debtors comes another verse that has become controversial in the modern era. People are allowed to lend money but not to charge usurious interest rates, and when they lend money, they must record the amount so that no disagreements will arise. The Quran says that the parties involved in the transaction should get someone else to write it down fairly. It specifies that the debtor (or the debtor's guardian, in case the debtor is incapable) is to dictate to the scribe and that he must tell the full amount of the debt. The Quran then specifies that the transaction must also be witnessed by two men, or by one man and two women in case two men are not available (2:282). All this care is taken to avoid inequity in lending practices. However, traditional interpreters also derive from this verse that women's testimony in court is worth only half that of men. Modern thinkers believe the requirement for two women in place of one man pertains only to circumstances, like those of seventh-century Arabia, in which most women were uneducated and unfamiliar with business transactions. Again, given the Quran's overall emphasis on human equality, most modern thinkers do not believe that the Quran dictates that women's testimony should always be equal to half that of men.

Justice, therefore – however it is interpreted in specific circumstances – is the defining feature of the ideal Islamic society, as evidenced in the Quranic refrain, "God loves the just." (5:42; 49:9; 60:8) Submitting (*islam*) to the will of God is often described as exerting every effort to implement the values revealed in scripture. Among the most popular passages summarizing Quranic values is the following:

> It is not a matter of piety that you turn your faces to the East or West [in prayer]. Righteous is the one who believes in God and the Last Day, the angels and Scripture and the prophets; gives wealth, however cherished, to relatives and orphans, the needy and travelers and beggars, and for freeing slaves; and prays and gives zakah. And [the righteous] fulfill their promises when they make them, and are patient in misfortune, hardship and trouble. These are the ones who are proven truthful and are pious. (2:177)

A society characterized by justice, wherein the well-being of the entire group is measured in terms of the well-being of its most vulnerable members, is the external manifestation of *islam*. The internal manifestation may be found in a set of virtues that form the Islamic conscience. Muslims are expected to be guided by the will of God in every encounter, every decision, every action. They are called to live their lives guided by *taqwa*, a term whose common English translation as "fear of God" or "righteousness" does not do it justice. Along with *iman* (belief in God) and *islam* (submission to the will of God), *taqwa* is one of Islam's quintessential virtues. Belief in God is considered essential for human beings to be able to overcome their innate insecurities and selfishness. It is also considered natural, an inborn instinct. Submission to the will of God is believed to be the proper response to recognition of God, indeed the only possible response. True recognition of God inevitably results in recognition that His will is in the best interests of humanity. Failure to accept the will of God indicates incomplete faith. But how to implement the will of God in all aspects of life is the challenge. No law book could prescribe correct actions for all possible situations. The challenge for human beings is to internalize the ideals of Islam as well as the motivation to realize them in daily life. This internalization of the desire to fulfill the will of God is the beginning of taqwa.

The Quran gives guidance on some specific matters, often describing a particular choice as "closer to taqwa" or "approximating taqwa." For example, in response to questions about divorce before consummation of a marriage, men are told that they should provide support for the divorced bride fairly, in accordance with their means, even if it is not required by the marriage agreement. That is called "closer to taqwa." (2:237) Likewise, believers are told that they must never let hatred for a people lead to unjust behavior. "Act justly, that is nearer to taqwa." (5:8) In general, people are told to help one another in the effort to achieve taqwa (5:2) and to "conspire for virtue and taqwa" (58:9; see Chapter 2, "Spirituality," for further discussion of taqwa).

Similarly, Muslims are called upon to be a "median" or balanced community (*ummat al-wasit*) "so that you may be witnesses to the people." (2:143) In yet another refrain of the Quran, believers are told that they are the best of communities in that they "enjoin honorable actions and forbid the objectionable" (*amr bi'l-ma'ruf wa nahiy 'an al-munkar*, 3:110; see also 3:104, 114; 7:157; 9:67, 71; 112; 22:41; 31:17). Believers are thus given the responsibility not simply to control their own behavior but to work actively against evil committed by others. They are reminded often of their responsibility to commit themselves fully to the effort to create a just society. They must struggle "in the way of God" (*jahadu fi sabil Allah*). "Strive with your wealth and your lives in the way of God" (9:41) is a common Quranic refrain. "Shall I point out a bargain that will save you from painful punishment? Believe in God and His messenger and strive in the path of God with your possessions and your lives." (61:11–12) The Arabic term for struggle is the verbal form of the noun *jihad*, a term that also means struggle. Performing the required prayers and fasting, regularly and sincerely, giving charity, and acting with honesty and compassion are all part of jihad. When the community is under attack, fighting the aggressors is also required, and becomes part of the virtuous struggle.[2] But the "greater jihad," according to Islamic tradition, consists of the daily effort to be the kind of person and create the kind of society envisioned by the Quran.

The task of fully submitting to the will of God is therefore all-consuming. It requires constant effort, but not because any single individual is expected to take more responsibility than s/he can manage. The Quran often counsels that God does not require from people anything beyond their strength (2:286; 6:152; 7:42; 23:62). People will be judged on their intentions: "God . . . will hold you responsible for what your hearts have earned." (2:226) Nor is any one group expected to be successful in the struggle to establish a just society in a given time or place; the community of believers as a whole has the responsibility to work toward that goal, by following the guidance given in the Quran and the model established by Prophet Muhammad in Medina as a guide. The Quran is the ultimate source of guidance for Muslims. Coming as it did after earlier revelations (the Torah and Gospels), the Quran is considered the final revelation. It was recorded very soon (within twenty years) after the Prophet's death in 632 CE, unlike Jewish and Christian scriptures which were not recorded until centuries after their revelation. Therefore, the Quran is believed to be free of the errors that crept into the previous scriptures. And Muhammad, the messenger who delivered the Quran, is considered the final prophet. As the Quran puts it, he is the "seal of the prophets" (*khatim al-nabiyyin*, 33:40), meaning that he is the last in the line of prophets that began with the creation of Adam. Humanity has received complete revelation; the task now is to implement its vision, to put it into practice. But Muhammad's role extends beyond the task of delivering revelation. His life is also a model for humanity of how to live every moment, and make every choice, in accordance with God's will. The way he lived his life is described by the Quran as the best example of Islam: "Indeed in the messenger of God is a good example for those who look to God and the Last day and remember God often." (33:22) Together, the Quran and the example (called the Sunna) set by Prophet Muhammad comprise the guidance Muslims need in their collective responsibility to establish justice.

However, following that guidance is not a simple matter of imitation. The great challenge lies in the fact that just as circumstances changed during the lifetime of Prophet Muhammad, circumstances continue to change, and that requires flexibility in determining ways to implement God's will. The most traditional interpreters might believe that following the Prophet's example means keeping society just as it was in the Prophet's time in Medina. For them, the challenge would be to prevent social change. The majority of Muslims, however, believe that the model established in the Quran and the Prophet's example describes ideals of human dignity and justice, and how they were maintained in the circumstances that existed during the Prophet's lifetime. Therefore, it is necessary to distinguish between the eternal ideals and the changeable or contingent circumstances. It is necessary to distinguish between prescriptions and descriptions so that the principles may be applied in new circumstances.

For example, the Quran provides a significant amount of legislation concerning the treatment of slaves. It allows the common practice of concubinage, but demands that slave women not be forced into sexual relations (24:33). The Quran acknowledges that slaves do not have the same legal standing as free people; instead, they are treated as minors for whom the owners are responsible. But it recommends that unmarried Muslims marry their slaves (24:32), indicating that it considers slaves and free people morally equal. It also instructs Muslims to allow their slaves to buy their freedom, and even to help them pay for it if possible (24:33). The Quran clearly recognizes that slavery is a source of inequity in society, since it frequently recommends freeing slaves, along with feeding and clothing the poor, as part of living a moral life (90:12–18) and a way to make up for offenses (5:90; 58:3). Yet despite its overall emphasis on human dignity and equality, the Quran does not abolish the institution of slavery. As in the days of the Hebrew Bible, slavery was an integral part of the economic system at the time the Quran was revealed; abolition of slavery would have required an overhaul of the entire socioeconomic system. Therefore, instead of abolishing slavery outright, virtually all interpreters agree that the Quran established an ideal toward which society should work (struggle): a society in which no one would be enslaved to another. Therefore, although slavery was permitted in the Quran, it is now banned in Muslim countries.

The principle demonstrated in this example is that there is a distinction between the reality of legal slavery in the Quran, and the moral recommendations concerning slavery. The former is considered a contingent circumstance, able to be changed. The latter reflects the eternal model of human dignity. At the time of the early Muslim community, the immediate emancipation of all slaves would have caused economic chaos – which obviously would not have been conducive to Islamic goals of well-being for all people. But the ideals toward which the community should strive were clearly set forth in this case. Applying the ideals in the modern world requires the abolition of slavery, a goal that has largely been achieved in the Muslim world.

The same kinds of distinctions arise in discussions of Islamic teaching on many social issues. For example, people concerned about the status of women often focus on the example discussed above in which the Quran explains that loans should be witnessed by two men or else by one man and two women. Given that the explanation for this ruling is that women may forget the details of the transaction ("so one may remind the other"), the following questions arise. Does this verse imply that women should always be unfamiliar with the details of finance and therefore their testimony on financial issues always in need of verification? Or does it mean that women's testimony on any issue in general would always need verification? Or does it mean that the testimony of anyone who is uneducated needs corroboration, and the verse simply used women as an example, so that the testimony of educated women should actually be considered reliable? As noted, although opinion on this issue is divided (as it is on the status of women in many religions), most modern commentators believe the Quran's essential egalitarianism indicates that the lack of economic skills in women in the Quran's discussion of lending practices is simply an example, not an eternal ideal. Similarly, the Quran and the Sunna provide guidance on equitable treatment for women in patriarchal society. Thus, the Quran specifies that men are responsible for women because "God has favored some people over others" and because they "spend their wealth" or support women (4:34). Women should therefore be obedient to men and may be disciplined for disobedience. Does this mean that men should always be in charge, or that whoever happens to be financially successful – male or female – should be responsible for the family and that if financial responsibility is shared, authority in the family should also be shared? Again, as in virtually all mainstream religions, traditional opinion is that men are divinely ordained to be responsible for public matters, including finances, while women are responsible primarily for private matters – including caring for the husband and nurturing children. Progressive thinkers opt for a more egalitarian interpretation of the Quran's view of the status of women. Both are equally Islamic, and both take inspiration from the example set by the early Muslim community.

The Early Muslim Community and the Pillars of Islam

Muslims involved in debates over how to establish justice in modern societies inevitably return to the model community established by Prophet Muhammad in the seventh century. That community was resoundingly successful in its effort to create a society characterized by justice, peace, and harmony. The decades of internal strife that had plagued Medina were over. Upon his arrival in Medina, the Prophet struck an agreement among the various tribes there and his community of Meccans. This agreement is recorded in history as the Constitution of Medina. According to the provisions of the agreement, all religious communities in Medina form a single community, "separate from other people."[3] They are to be mutually supportive, particularly in case of attack. Reflecting the Quran's teaching, Jews and Muslims are expected to maintain their own religious practices; disputes are to be referred to Prophet Muhammad and God. There were no Christian tribes in Medina, but later on, Christians and other religious groups were accorded religious freedom, based on the Quran's prohibition of compulsion in matters of religion (2:256) and on the precedent established in the Constitution of Medina. Prior to the establishment of the Islamic community in Medina, tribes had been the dominant form of social organization. Tribes were extended families, under the leadership of dominant males, and each was an autonomous unit. Although occasionally alliances would be formed through marriages, there was no effective precedent in the region for a social organization that included peoples of varying families and religious traditions cooperating in the pursuit of shared ideals.

The peace and prosperity of this community comprised of various tribes with differing religions living in harmony quickly attracted the attention of its neighbors. There had been some internal dissent. On three occasions local tribes were believed to have violated the constitution by conspiring with outsiders against the Medinan community. They were, therefore, expelled (in the first two cases), or executed (in the third case). Because all three of these tribes were Jewish, some people think that the community in Medina turned against Jews. In fact, some verses from the Quran referring to incidents such as these caution Muslims against trusting Jews and Christians. (For example, "O you who believe, do not take Jews and Christians for friends. They are friends of one another." 5:52) However, other Jewish tribes continued to live in peace in Medina. Furthermore, the majority of verses of the Quran, as noted above, endorse pluralism. The following verse is typical of the Quran's acceptance of Jews and Christians (among others): "Surely, those who have believed, and the Jews and the Sabians and the Christians, whoever believes in God and the Last Day and does good deeds need have no fear nor shall they grieve." (5:71) Therefore, most commentators agree that the verses criticizing other religions are directed at specific beliefs or actions, not against the groups as a whole.

Indeed, the model of inter-tribal harmony established at Medina seemed to be attractive to the surrounding communities. During the lifetime of the Prophet, most tribes of the Arabian peninsula accepted Islam and pledged their allegiance to the Prophet, making Muhammad the most powerful leader in the region. Within eight years of the Hijra, and after several battles, the Meccans also recognized the authority of the Prophet. The event was dramatic. In 628 it was revealed to Muhammad that he would pray in Mecca (48:27). He therefore set out with about one thousand unarmed pilgrims who also wanted to pray in Mecca. They were stopped outside the city at Hudaybiyyah by the Meccans. In order to preserve peace, the Prophet negotiated a ten-year truce, agreeing to postpone the pilgrimage for a year. But two years later the truce was violated and Muhammad marched on Mecca. He was met by the leader of Mecca's leading tribe, the Quraysh, who accepted Islam and negotiated peace. Granting amnesty to the city that had persecuted his community, Muhammad entered the city peacefully, and rededicated the Kaaba, the ancient shrine at the center of Mecca. According to the Quran, the Kaaba was originally built by Abraham and his son Ishmael to honor the one God. But the Kaaba had since been taken over by local tribes who had filled it with symbols and relics of their polytheistic religions. Local tribes made annual pilgrimages to Mecca, in combination with the city's annual trade fair and cultural events. When Prophet Muhammad returned to the Kaaba, he cleared the idols from the Kaaba and made it the focus of pilgrimage for Muslims.

The pilgrimage (*hajj*) is known as the fifth pillar or basic practice of Islam. The first pillar is the shahada, the pledging of commitment to God and the teachings of his prophet Muhammad. "I bear witness that there is no god (*ilah*) but the God (*al-ilah/*Allah) and Muhammad is the messenger of God." Anyone who sincerely commits to live according to this pledge is considered a Muslim.

The second pillar is prayer (*salat*). Muslims pray five times daily (at sunrise, midday, mid-afternoon, sunset, and nighttime). The prayers consist of recitations of verses of the Quran performed in a series of submissive postures (including bowing low from a kneeling position, so that the forehead touches the ground), and are meant to keep Muslims focused on the will of God in all aspects of life. Many people perform their prayers in mosques (*masajid*, "places of prostration"), although prayers may be performed anywhere that has been swept clean (symbolizing entering a state of purity). The prayer rug, a small carpet usually with a directional indicator to be pointed toward Mecca (the proper direction of prayer), is often used for this purpose. Some people substitute a piece of cloth or cardboard if they have no rug. Believers are instructed simply to precede prayer by washing (or symbolically washing, if no water is available), to prepare themselves spiritually to focus entirely on God. On Fridays the midday prayer should be performed communally in the mosque. At that time, the prayer leader (*imam*) often offers a sermon (*khutbah*) on the topic of his choice.

The third pillar is *zakah* (also spelled *zakat*), or charity. As noted above, all Muslims are required to be charitable; *zakah* requires all adult Muslims to give a share of their wealth annually for the support of the poor and to further the cause of Islam.

The fourth pillar is fasting (*sawm* or *siyyam*). All healthy Muslims past the age of puberty (i.e., neither the very young or very old, nor those who are sick, pregnant or nursing) are expected to fast from sunrise until sunset during the ninth month of the Islamic calendar (Ramadan). This is a very spiritual time, during which Muslims pray regularly and read the Quran, and focus on the equality of all people in their utter dependence on God. At the end of the month of fasting comes one of Islam's two major holidays, the breaking of the fast (Eid al-Fitr). Families and communities celebrate this feast for three days, sharing joyous meals and giving gifts to the children.

As noted, the Hajj is the fifth pillar. Muslims are obligated to make the pilgrimage at least once in their lifetimes if they are physically and financially able, during the month designated as "the month of pilgrimage" (*dhu al-hijja*). During that time pilgrims dress in simple clothes, removing any indicators of social rank, and together perform ceremonies designed to remind them of the founding of the Kaaba and their utter reliance on (submission to) God. The pilgrimage culminates in the feast of the sacrifice (Eid al-Adha), the second of Islam's major holidays. Sheep are slaughtered, symbolizing Abraham's sacrifice; the meat is then consumed and any excess is given to the poor.

The five pillars (*arkan*) are the basic practices of Islam. They structured Islamic life in Medina, as they continue to do today.

The pillars are simple practices designed to remind the believers constantly of their commitment to the divine will. They also focus attention on the core values of Islam: the equality of all human beings in the eyes of God and the responsibility of all believers to contribute to the well-being of society. Around these practices and core values, the early Muslim community was built and prospered. Following the rededication of the Kaaba in 630, Prophet Muhammad received overtures from tribes throughout the Arabian peninsula, accepting Islam and becoming part of the community, or pledging alliance with the Prophet. The Christian tribes among the bedouin (desert-dwelling nomadic herders) and Jewish tribes, many from the desert oases, generally kept their religious identities, as in Medina, while the polytheistic tribes generally became Muslim. By the time of the Prophet's death, the Islamic community based in Medina was the most vibrant moral, social, and political force in the Arabian peninsula.

The Successors ("Caliphs")

When Prophet Muhammad died after a brief illness in 632, his followers were distraught. Abu Bakr, one of his closest companions, declared to them, "If anyone worships Muhammad, [know that] Muhammad is dead. But if anyone worships God, [know that] God is alive and does not die." His goal was to refocus attention on the message, rather than on the messenger. Muslims maintain the deepest respect for Muhammad and continue to be inspired by his example. But he was a man, a servant of God, as Abu Bakr reminded the community on this sad occasion when he repeated the Quranic verse, "Muhammad is only a messenger; messengers have died before him. When he dies will you turn your back on him? Whoever turns back does no harm to God but God will reward the grateful." (3:144) The believers were comforted and inspired by this; they were to maintain their commitment to the will of God, taking individual responsibility for their actions. But what about the community as a whole? Who would lead them?

A number of possibilities were suggested. Many of the nomadic tribes around Medina felt that their allegiance had been to Prophet Muhammad. For them his death meant the end of their affiliation; they indicated their withdrawal from the alliance by ending their zakah payments to Medina. Many others believed that in the absence of Muhammad's central leadership, the tribes and communities – including Mecca – should revert to local leadership. After all, the Prophet had not discussed political systems nor specified a political order to take over after his death. But Abu Bakr and other close companions of the Prophet were convinced that Muslims had to remain a single community – not just morally unified through commitment to monotheism and the message of Prophet Muhammad, but politically unified, as well. Their opinion prevailed. The companions of the Prophet pledged allegiance to Abu Bakr as leader of the community, referring to him as the Prophet's representative (*khalifah* or "caliph"). He was first among equals, leading through consultation (*shura*) with other elders in the community, just as the Prophet had done and in accordance with the Quranic directive: "So pardon them and ask forgiveness for them and consult with them on the conduct of affairs." (3:159)

Abu Bakr then led the community in a momentous decision: to bring the tribes that had seceded back into the community by force, if necessary. The Quran stipulates that "there is no compulsion in religion." (2:256) It reinforces that position elsewhere. For example, when discussing preaching to People of the Book, Muhammad is instructed:

> If they argue with you, say my followers and I have surrendered ourselves to God. And say to those who have received Scripture

and to the illiterate: "Have you surrendered [to God]?" If they surrender [to God], then they are rightly guided, and if they turn away, then it is your duty only to preach. (3:20)

This verse, in fact, guides Muslim attitudes toward proselytizing. Nevertheless, the decision was made to enforce the political unity of the believers militarily. The seceders were declared apostates, and the campaigns against them are still known as the wars of apostasy (*riddah*). The decision to enforce unity among believers had a significant effect on the development of Islam. It established a policy that resulted in one of the most extraordinary political expansions in history. By the time Abu Bakr died in 634, all the tribes of the Arabian peninsula had been brought into the Islamic political orbit. Under Abu Bakr's successors, Umar and Uthman, the Islamic army set out to rid Syria and Mesopotamia (Iraq) of the hated Byzantine and Sasanian empires. (Further implications of the decision to enforce political unity will be discussed in Chapter 4.)

At that time the Middle East was in the final throes of devastating competition between the Eastern Roman Empire (the Christian Byzantines) and the Sasanian Persian Empire (Zoroastrian). The Byzantines had occupied coastal Syria, which at that time included parts of the present states of Syria, Lebanon, Jordan, Israel, the Palestinian territories, and Egypt. The Sasanians of Persia (called Iran since the 1930s) controlled most of present-day Iraq. After decades of debilitating wars, both empires were weakened internally. Arab tribes on the frontiers of the empires readily accepted the leadership of the Muslims. The formerly great Roman and Persian armies were defeated with little trouble.

The Byzantines had long persecuted their Jewish subjects, as well as those Christians who rejected Orthodoxy. For these groups Muslim rule was especially welcome. Those who accepted Islam were taught the basics of the religion by Quran reciters. But Christians and Jews were free to retain their religious identity.

In addition, the taxes imposed by the Muslims were initially lighter than those of the older empires and, unlike many conquering armies, the Arab Muslims were not allowed to take control of the conquered lands for personal use. Thus, Jerusalem was liberated from Roman rule in 636, Mosul was taken from the Persians in 641, and the Romans were defeated in Alexandria by 646. The last Sasanian ruler was killed in 651, the Roman fleet destroyed by Muslim sea power in 655, and the Muslim state headquartered in Medina became the most powerful in the region.

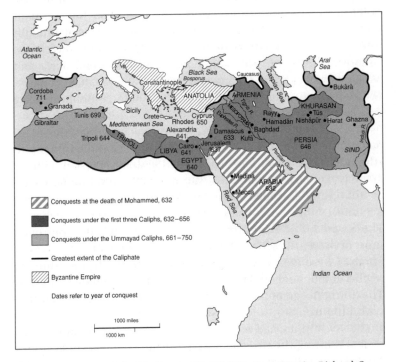

Map 1 Expansion of the Muslim world 632–750. From Martin, Richard C., *Islamic Studies: A History of Religious Approach* (Upper Saddle River, NJ: Prentice Hall, 1996).

Early Ideological Disputes

The phenomenal expansion of Islamic sovereignty was a result of the early decision by the Prophet's successors that Islamic unity must be assured through political unity. But political unity proved virtually impossible to maintain as Islamic sovereignty continued to spread. Efforts to enforce that unity engendered conflicts that called into question the very nature of the Islamic community. A recurring theme in the early conflicts was the tribal nature of Arab culture. In pre-Islamic times, tribes were the basic unit of social organization, and each tribe had its own values, sources of authority, organization, rituals, and beliefs – all of which would later be identified as aspects of religion.[4] This is the context for understanding the gravity with which the question of apostasy was treated in early Islam. To change one's religion was not simply a matter of spiritual persuasion as we see it today. It was effectively to change one's political loyalty, a potentially treasonous act. Christianity had attempted to supersede this religio-political identity. Jesus' command "to render unto Caesar the things that are Caesar's, and unto God the things that are God's" (Mt. 22:21) was meant to allow people to follow their religious consciences without it calling into question their political loyalty.[5] People could be Christian in the Roman Empire without being considered subversives. But the equation of religious and political loyalty was re-imposed when Christianity was declared the official religion of the Roman Empire. The Quran's teaching of religious freedom was in effect a return to the ideal espoused by Jesus. It was a reassertion of the independence of religious and ethnic identity. This ethic was institutionalized in the Constitution of Medina, when Prophet Muhammad included Jews and Muslims in the same political community. Again stressing the struggle against tribalism, the Prophet said in his final speech that Arabs have no superiority over non-Arabs.

Nevertheless, the tribal tendency to equate religious and ethnic/national identity was so well entrenched that it reemerged soon after the Prophet's death. Umar, the second caliph, determined that only Islam would be allowed in the Arabian peninsula, the Quran's teaching and the Prophet's example of religious tolerance notwithstanding. Under his administration, Jews and Christians were expelled, so that all Arabs (meaning those who live in the Arabian peninsula; later on, the term "Arab" would apply to all Arabic speakers) were Muslim; thus, religious and ethnic identity were rejoined. Umar's successor, Uthman, reasserted a tribal tendency that challenged even other Arab Muslims. He headed an administration staffed almost exclusively by members of his own Meccan clan, the Umayyads, resulting in numerous protests. Umar's policy concerning land taxation also resulted in protests. It stipulated that revenues from conquered land would be sent to Medina for the benefit of the central administration, the conquering Arab soldiers and their families. Muslims from outside Medina felt that their land taxes should be used locally. Policies such as these seemed to violate Islamic norms of justice and equality, and resentment mounted. Umar was murdered by a Persian slave in 644. Uthman continued Umar's policies, resulting in more discontent. Minor rebellions broke out in towns established solely for Arab Muslim conquerors in Egypt (al-Fustat) and Iraq (Kufah). In 656, rebellious Muslims from Egypt marched to Medina and assassinated Uthman.

The growing discontent found a champion in Ali, the Prophet's companion, cousin, and son-in-law. Following Uthman's death, Ali was chosen by majority opinion within the community to be the next "leader of the believers." He was well respected and had been a contender for the office since the beginning, but he was not as senior as Abu Bakr, Umar, and Uthman. However, a group of Ali's supporters believed that Ali should have been chosen as the first caliph, because they believed that the Prophet had designated him as his successor. This group believed that the first three caliphs were usurpers and that Ali was the first legitimate caliph. Eventually, this group would be called the "partisans of Ali" – *shiat Ali*, or simply Shiah (or Shii, in adjective form, or Shiites, in anglicized form). (The development of Shii thought will be discussed further in Chapter 3.)

Not all Ali's supporters believed that his legitimacy rested on the Prophet's designation. Many supported him because of his piety, wisdom, and courage, particularly in this time of civil strife. These included a group later identified as the Kharijis (or Kharijites, "the Seceders"), who believed that Uthman's nepotism (staffing his administration with members of his own family) was such a serious violation of Islamic principles that he was no longer eligible even to be called a Muslim, let alone a caliph. But Ali also had enemies. Chief among them were Aishah, widow of the Prophet and daughter of the first caliph Abu Bakr; and Muawiyah, the governor of Damascus appointed by Uthman. Aishah, who held personal grudges against Ali, led a rebellion against him near Basra (in Iraq, near Kufah, where Ali had established his headquarters) in 656. Ali's troops easily defeated her troops (which she personally led). Muawiyah challenged Ali to find and punish the assassins of his kinsman Caliph Uthman. When he did not, Muawiyah led an army against him (657). On the verge of defeat, Muawiyah's troops asked for arbitration, which Ali granted. The arbitration allowed Muawiyah to maintain his post in Damascus. Unfortunately, this effort at reconciliation cost Ali the support of the Kharijis. In 661 Ali was assassinated by one of them, leaving the caliphate to the Umayyad family in Damascus. (For further discussion of the Kharijis, see Chapter 4.)

Conclusion

The violent end of three of the first four caliphs reflects the turmoil that gripped the Muslim community after the death of Prophet Muhammad. The community had the Quran and his example (the Sunna) to guide them, but still they were left with an enormous challenge. As noted above, the Quran is not a lawbook but a guide and source of moral inspiration. It reaffirms the covenant accepted by Abraham, the "trust" that human beings accepted at creation, the agreement that God offers eternal reward to those who take up the struggle to re-create in society the equality all human beings share in the eyes of God. But there are no formulae for ensuring that justice is always done. That is the part human beings have to figure out, each community and every generation, in an endless variety of circumstances. They must evaluate the circumstances in light of moral guidance, and then determine what actions and institutions are most conducive to justice in those specific circumstances. And they must do it in cooperation with others, since no one can create justice alone. The Quran describes its guidance as very clear, and it is; there is no doubt about what the goals of a just society are. But it is very difficult to figure out how to achieve those goals "on the ground" – as anyone who is engaged in social activism knows.

The early Muslim community was faced with the enormous challenge of institutionalizing justice not only in their own communities, but sharing those ideals and institutions with others who had suffered injustice just as they had. It is certainly to their credit that they relieved the region of the heavy burden of Roman and Persian imperialism. That conflicts would arise over the practical matters of governance is not surprising. It is natural that among tribal people, some would believe leadership should stay within their own community, while people outside that community would reject that model of leadership. It is just as natural that among moralizing people, many would believe that leadership should be based on piety, and many would rebel against rulers deemed unjust. In reality, the early years of Islam reflect both the benefits and the difficulties encountered in the transition from a community whose security is based on tribal bonds of mutual and unquestioned loyalty, to a community committed to justice on a global scale. This is a struggle that continues to this day. Like people of many other faiths, Muslims continue to explore the implications of working for justice in a pluralist society. Is salvation reserved only for Baptists, or Catholics, or Jews, or Muslims? Must we separate religious beliefs from political convictions in order to be able to live peacefully with people of other faiths? Indeed, can we separate the two? Does accepting the legitimacy of other faiths require abandoning one's own, or a "willing suspension of disbelief"? These are questions that confront all religions today. They are the same kinds of questions that the early Muslims struggled with.

The fact that there was conflict reflects the complexity of the problems faced and the depth of commitment on the part of the participants. In the context of Islamic history, it does not detract from the valiance of their efforts. Although Shii Muslims continue to believe that Ali was the first legitimate caliph, the majority of Muslims, the Sunnis, believe that the first four caliphs were "rightly guided" (*al-rashidun*). They look to this period as one in which the Quran's moral challenge dominated Islamic life. The Muslim community, with all its conflicts and failings, extended every effort "in the way of God" (*fi sabil Allah*). Even today, traditionalist Muslims look to this community as an example of truly Islamic life, and accept some of the precedents established during this period (such as the death penalty for apostasy). Reform-minded Muslims, on the other hand, respect the efforts of this early community, while rejecting some of its precedents, and look to the Quran and Sunna for guidance in facing the challenges of modern life.

Whether Sunni or Shii, traditionalist or reformist, all Muslims consider this period the time during which Islamic ideals were established. Although the Shiis do not accept Abu Bakr, Umar, and Uthman as legitimate leaders of the community, and modern-day reformers reject some of their specific judgments, all Muslims believe that this community took up the challenge of the *khalifah*. This term, appropriated in the political sphere to mean "successor" of the Prophet, actually has a much broader meaning in the Quran, where it is used twice. In a famous passage that encapsulates much of Islamic teaching, the Quran says that God created humanity to be His *khalifah* (2:30). Clearly the meaning here is "steward" or "deputy." Human beings were put here to be responsible for maintaining the equality in which all were created. Elsewhere, the Quran describes God addressing King David as His khalifah who, as such, must judge in all things with honor and justice (38:26). Despite its weaknesses and conflicts, the early Muslim community accepted the challenge of stewardship and struggled to enjoin good and prevent evil. It is that legacy that has continued to inspire Muslims throughout the ages.

Chapter 2

Pursuit of Knowledge in the Service of God and Humanity: The Golden Age

The conflicts that gripped the Muslim community during the caliphate of Ali interrupted the spread of Islamic sovereignty. But following his death and the establishment of the seat of Islamic government in Damascus in 661, expansion resumed with continued success. After replacing Roman rule in Egypt, Muslim forces pushed across North Africa. Joined by Berber (and indigenous North African) converts, the Arabs crossed the straits from Africa to Andalusia (southern Spain), ascending the mountain to which their leader Tariq gave his name ("Gibraltar" comes from the Arabic *jabal tariq*, Tariq's Mountain or Mt. Tariq). Within just one century of Prophet Muhammad's death, Muslims had established Islamic sovereignty throughout much of Spain, which remained Islamic in some areas until the Reconquista was complete in 1492. The Muslims' advance into Europe was stopped in Gaul (France) by Charles Martel at the Battle of Tours in 732.

In the East, Islamic rule was established throughout former Sasanian lands, all the way to the Indus River and the border of China by the eighth century. Islam continued its eastward spread through the fourteenth century, when traders and itinerant preachers traveled to China, South Asia, and Southeast Asia, establishing roots for the current Islamic countries of Indonesia and Malaysia. Significant portions of the Indian subcontinent were ruled by Muslims from the thirteenth century until the British took control in 1857. It was, indeed, a phenomenal expansion. And with it came the development of a highly sophisticated culture. Marked by openness and creativity, it was inspired by the Quran and the Prophet Muhammad's example, and still serves as a model of what truly Islamic society can achieve.

Institutions

As noted in the previous chapter, the subjects of the Byzantine (Eastern Roman) and the Sasanian Persian empires generally welcomed Muslim rule since it allowed respite from religious persecution and resulted in generally lower taxes. This reflected the rationale for the expansion of Islamic rule; Muslims sincerely believed that Islam was divinely ordained to bring peace and relief from oppression to humanity. Thus, when Muslims approached a new community, they offered the protection of Islam. Those who chose not to accept Islam as their religion were offered treaties; they could pay a tribute in return for the right to retain religious freedom and internal autonomy. Those who refused either to accept Islam or agree to live in peace with Muslims through treaty agreements were forced to submit by means of military action.

This method of conquest resulted in a division of the world into three parts: *dar al-Islam*, *dar al-'ahd* (or *sulh*), and *dar al-harb*. *Dar al-Islam* refers to those territories in which the Islamic law prevails. *Dar al-'ahd* (region of covenant) and *dar al-sulh* (region of truce) were both regions whose leaders had agreed to pay the Muslim leaders a tax and to protect the rights of any Muslims or Muslim allies who lived there, but who otherwise maintained their autonomy, including their own legal systems. *Dar al-harb* was a region whose leaders had made no such agreement and where, therefore, Muslims and their allies were neither guaranteed the right to live by Islamic law nor were protected by it. For this reason it was called "region of warfare." This does not mean that such regions were automatically subject to attack by Muslims, since *harb* is not legitimate warfare in Islam. When warfare is sanctioned in Islam, it is called jihad, struggle "in the way of God" that is carried out through military means and according to strict rules of engagement. This is the only kind of warfare allowed under Islamic law. Referring to a region as *dar al-harb* reflects the perception that the region itself was warlike and Muslims were not safe there.

Through this system, the Muslim world, a region where Muslims made up the vast majority, was transformed into the Islamic world – a world dominated by Muslim institutions but including significant non-Muslim populations. Such an enormous and complex world required administration beyond the simple model established by the Prophet and his earliest successors. That model had been relatively informal, and based on direct interaction of community members and leaders. In the expanded Islamic empire, more sophisticated administrative systems became necessary.

A system of taxation was the first order of business. In general, the Muslim conquerors allowed local authorities to collect taxes according to their established customs. Since some of the newly acquired territories had been variously administered according to Roman law, Persian law, and other regional systems, the system of taxation under Muslim rule became quite complex. Iraq, for example, was conquered through military victory over the drained Sasanian forces, with the help of local Arab tribes. The native Arabs were left in control of taxation and followed the Sasanian tradition, which included both a land tax and a poll tax (tax based on the number of people living there). But the poll tax varied according to the degree of wealth among the populace, except for the aristocracy, who were exempt from the poll tax. In Syria, where Islamic dominance was achieved largely by treaty, tax collection was left to the discretion of the native administrators. They followed in basic outline the fiscal system of the previous Roman overlords, which was even more complex than the Persian system.[1] The central treasury therefore had to be very sophisticated to keep track of all these differing systems of taxation.

Law

Of far greater importance than taxation, however, was the institutionalization of law, since it regulated Islamic practice overall. In this area, too, the Muslim practice of leaving in place systems that had dominated a region prior to the coming of Islam was evident. In accordance with Islamic principles and the Prophet's practice, religious freedom was the norm throughout Islamic realms. The right accorded to Jews in the Constitution of Medina to maintain their religious and legal systems was extended to Christians and later to Zoroastrians, Hindus, and Buddhists. But what about those who chose to become Muslim? The inclusion of vast new populations into the community of Muslims meant that an expanded legal system had to be developed. According to tradition, Prophet Muhammad stipulated that local customs were to be tolerated, as long as they did not interfere with Islamic principles. But someone had to determine what was or was not in accordance with Islamic principles. Muslims had to develop a legal system that would be flexible enough to function effectively throughout Islam's expansive and diverse realms, but rigorous enough to maintain a distinctive Islamic identity.

In the days of the first caliphs, when the system was still relatively informal and modeled on the practice of the Prophet, Muslims were simply expected to follow Islamic practice, including regular prayer, charity, fasting, and pilgrimage. Regarding other issues of governance and in matters of conflict, the Quran had stipulated that Muslims were to "obey God and the Messenger and those among you in authority." (4:62) But beyond that, the Quran had specified no particular form of government. Muhammad's early successors, therefore, as his "successors" or "representatives" (caliphs) and "leaders of the believers," attempted to follow the Prophet's example by living lives of piety and arbitrating disputes when they arose. But with the expansion of Islamic sovereignty, this informal practice proved insufficient, and was gradually transformed into a legal system that could function independent of the head of state.

The first major transition in Islamic governance came with the assumption of power by the Umayyads, descendants of a powerful Meccan family. Although some people had argued that Ali should be appointed successor to the Prophet because of his family relationship with him, hereditary leadership was not the dominant pattern in Arab society. But after the Umayyad Muawiyah was recognized as caliph, his family kept control of that office until a revolution ousted them in 750. During the Umayyads' reign, a distinction between specifically religious and the coercive/executive levels of political authority developed. Damascus became the political or administrative capital of the empire while Mecca remained the religious/legislative center. But still there was no theory upon which the government was based. As noted, the caliphs left in place whatever systems had prevailed before the Muslim conquest. For other legal issues, the Umayyads introduced into their administration a new office, that of judges (qadis). These were political appointees with varied administrative responsibilities, including police and treasury work, but generally charged with settling disputes in accordance with local custom and Islamic principles. They were allowed a great deal of latitude, exercising their own judgment about what was permissible in view of Islamic principles and administrative necessities.

However, it soon became apparent, to some people at least, that Umayyad leadership no longer was the model of wisdom and piety that Islamic leadership ideally symbolized. This recognition gave rise to opposition groups, including scholars who objected that Umayyad policies violated Islamic principles. In the process of discussing which actions and policies were Islamic and which were not, scholars actually developed the formal theories of Islamic law that became the core of Islamic life.[2] When Christianity became politically institutionalized in Rome in the fourth century, it devised a way to determine who was really a Christian by developing a "creed," a list of beliefs. Whoever accepted the beliefs of Christianity was a Christian and therefore a full citizen; those who rejected Christian beliefs were non-Christian and considered a threat to the Christian community. That is why the major discipline in Christianity is theology, a discussion of beliefs. In Islam, on the other hand, just as in Judaism, the emphasis is not so much on belief as on actions. Belief is important; correct behavior is assumed to be based on correct belief. But the critical point of religious identity is based on the discipline that deals with practice, and that is law. This does not mean that Islam became legalistic, however; like Judaic law, Islamic law is not simply a code of injunctions enforceable in a courtroom. As modern Islamic scholar Fazlur Rahman put it, Islamic law is "an endless discussion on the duties of a Muslim rather than a neatly formulated code or codes."[3] Law was therefore central to Islamic life in terms of daily life and religious practice, as well as state administration.

By the mid-eighth century, there was a discernible body of scholars who were popularly regarded as having the authority to identify and interpret the sources of Islamic law. They fell into schools of thought that generally developed according to regional practice. In Medina, for example, a school of Islamic legal thought developed based on local practice and in view of the interpretations of scripture and reports (hadiths) from the local people about what the Prophet said or did (his normative practice or "Sunna"). This body of ideas about practice was expressed in the work of Malik ibn Anas (d. 796), and is known as the Maliki school of law. Another center, with different local customs and different hadith reports, grew up in Kufa (in Iraq): the school of Abu Hanifa (d. 767), largely developed by his students Abu Yusuf (d. 798) and al-Shaybani (d. 804), and known as the Hanafi school. The development of these schools was essentially democratic; decisions about what was proper practice, in accordance with the Quran and the Prophet's example, were based on local consensus (*ijma*). In cases where there were no apparently applicable precedents in the Quran or Sunna, legal scholars used their discretion to determine the implications of revelation for the questions at hand. They practiced *ijtihad*, the name given to this interpretive work.

The Umayyads lost control of the caliphate when they were overthrown by the Abbasid family in 750 CE. As members of the opposition to the Umayyads, the legal scholars (*fuqaha'*) were naturally favored by the Abbasids. The new ruling family appointed these scholars as judges, rather than simply calling upon loyal functionaries as the Umayyads had done. This represented a significant step in the formalization of Islamic law. As legal historian N. J. Coulson put it, "The legal scholars were publicly recognized as the architects of an Islamic scheme of state and society which the Abbasids had pledged themselves to build, and under this political sponsorship the schools of law developed rapidly."[4] The scholars began to identify weaknesses in the system and the need for greater rigor in legal thought. Thus, a third school of Islamic law developed around the idea that legal reasoning should be consistent throughout the Islamic world. This was not an argument for uniform practice or judgments, only for agreement upon the sources of Islamic law and the ways to achieve sound legal rulings in cases for which no precedent could be found. It was an argument for procedural continuity, reflecting a growing awareness that regardless of the shifting political winds, the core of Islamic unity was in law. The school that emerged from this movement was named for its energetic founder, Muhammad ibn Idris al-Shafii (d. 820 CE). It is called the Shafii school of legal thought.

Al-Shafii had traveled to the major cities in the Muslim world, and noticed significant variations in legal reasoning. He set out to achieve consistency in legal procedures by articulating clearly the roots of Islamic law and their rank in terms of priority. For al-Shafii, as for all other Muslims, the first source is the Quran. In cases for which the Quran offers no specific judgment, the next source of guidance is the practice of Prophet Muhammad, the Sunna. But at the time of al-Shafii, the process by which the Sunna was communicated was still largely informal, based on the opinions of educated people about the Prophet's principles or ways of making decisions. Al-Shafii attempted to formalize the Sunna by equating it with credible hadith reports of what the Prophet said or did in specific circumstances. As a result, the concept of the Sunna was eventually restricted to specific examples of the Prophet's behavior. These could concern personal matters with no significant legal implications, such as how to clean one's teeth and whether or not to shave, as well as matters with important legal significance, such as how to conduct business or deal with poverty. In either case, these precedents became models to be imitated. And once they achieved such an important place in Islamic administration, the process of collecting, verifying, and codifying hadith reports began in earnest. By the ninth century, there were two collections of reports that were considered "sound" (*sahih*, meaning that the people who reported them had been scrutinized and found trustworthy, the contents of the reports were in keeping with Quranic teaching, etc.) and therefore authoritative. Those were the collections of Bukhari and Muslim (a name). Four other collections were considered valuable sources of insight concerning the Prophet and/or the Quran, but not as authoritative as the collections of Bukhari and Muslim. (The Shiis also have hadith collections, verified by virtue of transmission through Ali and his descendants.)

The third source of law for al-Shafii was the consensus of the community. The Prophet is reported to have asserted that his community would never agree on an error, and group consensus has therefore always been important in Islam. But al-Shafii concluded that only the consensus of the entire Islamic community should be considered authoritative, not just consensus within the various regions. And by the time he was working, given the extent the Islamic community had reached, full consensus was virtually impossible to attain. Therefore, al-Shafii believed it was preferable to follow precedent as much as possible. The third source of Islamic law, then, became judgments that had been reached by consensus of earlier generations about the meaning and application of the Quran. Independent reasoning (*ijtihad*), the fourth source of Islamic law, could be practiced only as a final resort, and it too was circumscribed. The intellectual effort to determine the implications of the Quran and Sunna was to be carried out through syllogistic reasoning, or reasoning by analogy (*qiyas*), rather than the more informal ijtihad based on personal opinion (*ray*).

Al-Shafii's school of jurisprudence remained only one of several within the Islamic system. A fourth school of thought was developed by one of his students, Ahmad ibn Hanbal (d. 855). Called the Hanbali school of legal thought, it places even greater emphasis on precedent than Shafii's school, although it also allows greater freedom in the use of ijtihad. Shii Muslims would develop a school of legal reasoning as well, known as the Jafari school. Nonetheless, al-Shafii came to be known as the "architect of Islamic law" because his work consolidated Islamic legal thought into a recognizable discipline at the core of Islamic life.[5] From his time on, a Muslim was officially defined as one who follows Islamic law.[6]

The systemization of legal administration gave the Islamic world a basic structure that has endured to this day. The Maliki, Hanafi, Shafii, Hanbali, and Jafari schools of legal thought still characterize the Islamic landscape worldwide. Each tends to predominate in specific regions: Maliki law in North and West Africa; Hanafi in areas formerly under Ottoman control and India; Shafii in Indonesia, Malaysia, and the Philippines; Hanbali in Saudi Arabia and Qatar; and Jafari in Shii regions like Iran. But the schools of thought differ relatively little and are, in fact, mutually acceptable. For example, all Muslims accept the five-part division of actions into those considered required (the five pillars), those recommended (such as giving charity above and beyond the required zakah), those considered neutral (such as smoking, according to most Muslims), those that are discouraged (such as divorce), and those that are forbidden (such as consuming intoxicants, eating pork, gambling). Actions in the first category are believed to be rewarded, and willful failure to perform them is punishable. Actions that fall into the second category are rewarded, but failure to perform them will not bring punishment. Actions considered to be neutral bring neither reward nor punishment. Those who avoid discouraged actions will benefit from their abstinence, and those who perform forbidden (*haram*) actions will be punished.

The classic formulations of Islamic law, accepted by all schools of thought, reflect the Quranic ethic of punishment by retaliation (*qisas*) for physical offenses, from assault to homicide. The person who strikes a physical blow is subject to whatever offense he has committed. As the Quran says, "A life for a life, an eye for an eye, and a nose for a nose, and an ear for an ear, and a tooth for a tooth, and for [other] injuries, fair retaliation." (5:46) The victim or the victim's family may choose to accept compensation (*diyah*) instead, and this is encouraged by the Quran. (The foregoing verse continues: "And whoever waives the right to this in charity, it will be an atonement [for sins].") There is another class of crime for which Islamic law has established specified mandatory punishments (*hadd*; pl. *hudud*), provided the perpetrator acted in full control of his senses and with full knowledge of his offenses, and that strict rules of evidence can be met. These hudud punishments include capital punishment for apostasy, highway robbery, what we now call terrorism (i.e., crimes against random victims), and illicit sex between married people; amputation of the hand for theft; and whipping for illicit sex between unmarried people or legal minors, or for drinking. (See Chapter 5 for further discussion of terrorism.) The rules of evidence required for these crimes are indeed strict. For example, conviction of adultery requires substantiation by four adult male eyewitnesses. Although such punishments seem harsh, they are considered primarily deterrent and, in fact, have proven to be effective in that regard. Most Muslims also believe that the hudud punishments are applicable only in conditions where high social standards have been met. They are not applicable in conditions of widespread ignorance, poverty, or social instability. Throughout history there are very few reports of the punishments actually being administered.

In traditional Islamic law, the courts are used to decide any issues other than physical injury or death, and those requiring hudud punishments. These include detailed laws concerning transactions (sales, rentals, loans, gifts to charitable foundations [*waqf*, pl. *awqaf*], etc.), family law (such as marriage, divorce, guardianship, custody), and laws of inheritance. In the traditional Islamic court, the judge (*qadi*) is given significant latitude. He may ask for an authoritative opinion (*fatwa*) from a professional legal scholar (*mufti*), but is not required to do so. Individuals may seek legal representation but in general are expected to state their cases personally. The judge may decide whether the plaintiff or the defendant bears the burden of proof, upon which the prosecutor must produce two witnesses (for most cases). If the evidence is unconvincing, the defendant is given the opportunity to swear innocence by a sacred oath. If the defendant refuses to offer such an oath, the case is decided in favor of the plaintiff.

In the modern era, traditional Islamic civil and criminal law was largely replaced by European legal codes during the period of colonization. Only matters considered private in European culture – those concerning family law – were left to Islamic courts. This has led to an interesting dynamic. Because of the centrality of law to Islamic society, there was a strong sense that the Europeans were stripping Islamic society of its identity. As a result, there was a tendency to safeguard traditional Islamic legal codes whenever possible. We will discuss in greater detail in Chapters 4 and 5 the tension this tendency has created in the modern era between reformers and traditionalists. Despite such tensions, however, Islamic law continues to represent the unifying element of diverse Islamic societies. Throughout the numerous political upheavals that have marked Islamic history, Islamic law has provided a sense of unity and allowed the Muslim community to remain coherent. Scholars, far more than rulers, are considered the symbols of Islamic unity.

A good illustration of this phenomenon is found in the adventures of Ibn Battutah, the fourteenth-century world traveler, Islam's precursor to Marco Polo. From his home in Tangier, Ibn Battutah traveled throughout the Muslim world, including all of North Africa; the Arab, Turkish, and Persian Middle East; the Maldive Islands, Sri Lanka, Bengal, and as far as China. His diary, still available, records that as a legal scholar he was welcomed in town after town all along his route, and given fine hospitality and respectful audiences. In the modern era, instant communications have made such international travel and personal contact unnecessary. Yet it is still the religio-legal scholars who have the potential to appeal well beyond their ethnic, national, and sectarian origins. As we will see in Chapters 4 and 5, scholars, more than politicians, have influenced events in the Islamic world from North Africa to Southeast Asia.

Political Structure

There is no characteristic political system in Islam. A government is not marked as Islamic based on the nature of its executive authority. Throughout history, Muslims have devised numerous political systems, from simple tribal groups led by elders (sheikhs); to empires ruled by caliphs, sultans, or shahs (kings);

to constitutional democracies and military dictatorships. What is required for political legitimacy in Islam is that whatever executive or administrative system exists, the law of the land must be based on Islamic sources. This was explicitly articulated in the eleventh century by Shafii scholar al-Mawardi (d. 1058). In a work entitled *Al-Ahkam al-Sultaniyya* (The Rules of Government) he explains that the duties of the political leaders fall into three categories: defense, treasury, and executive.[7] He is to defend the community from attack (article 3), maintain frontier defenses (article 5), and wage war against those who refuse to either become Muslim or enter into treaty with Muslims (article 6). Regarding economic responsibility, he is to collect both the alms payments (zakah) required of all Muslims and the legitimate spoils of wars (article 7). He must fairly determine and pay salaries from the treasury (article 8), and make sure those he appoints manage the treasury honestly (article 9). But most importantly, the ruler must make sure that the established principles of religion are safeguarded (article 1), and that legal judgments and penalties are enforced (articles 2 and 4). In other words, the ruler's authority is strictly executive/coercive. This position was reinforced by the great fourteenth-century Hanbali scholar Ibn Taymiyya (d. 1328) who said that the form of government can vary from time to time and place to place, depending upon custom and circumstance. But legal authority – articulating and adjudicating the law – remains not only distinct from executive administration. Legal authority is also of primary importance; the ruler can be any of a number of kinds, but as long as he makes sure an Islamic legal system is maintained, the government is legitimate.

In the medieval period, as the wealth of the Islamic empire increased, the office of the ruler became increasingly absolute in matters that concerned him. In fact, later Abbasid caliphs adopted the pre-Islamic Persian model of kingship in which the monarch was considered "the shadow of God on earth." However, the matters that concerned the caliph were not generally those that concerned the general population. It is ironic that despite the caliph's absolute power, classical Islamic government allowed for unprecedented freedom among the populace at large. Other than collecting taxes, the government did not interfere in the daily affairs of society. People were born, educated, married; they made their livings and bequeathed their wealth; they engaged in trade and other kinds of business – all without interference from the central government. Virtually all of daily life was under the purview of Islamic law, articulated and administered by legal scholars who operated for the most part independent of the central government.

It is often said that in Islam there is no distinction between politics and religion. This claim is misleading, however. It is true that Islam does not distinguish between political and religious values. The values that guide political or public life are the same as those that guide personal or private life. But in terms of administrative structure, Islamic law was quite separate from the executive branch. The executive branch had the authority to appoint judges, of course, but the judges were trained in institutions that were autonomous. In a system that bears striking similarities to our modern separation of powers, Muslim legal scholars maintained their autonomy through sources of income independent of government control. Their independence was maintained through a system of charitable foundations, called *awqaf* (singular: *waqf*), that have throughout history been at the core of Islamic civil society. A waqf is a kind of trust fund, a gift or bequest of property or the proceeds from a business to benefit society. People could give money or various business funds to establish something as small as a local fountain or as large as a hospital. Mosques are common beneficiaries of waqf trusts, and such endowments often include the education and support of legal scholars. These endowments had to be legally registered and were bound by the law of perpetuity; they could not revert to private use but had to continue to be used for charitable purposes as specified in their original charters. Waqf endowments were administered privately, by someone designated as the trustee at the time of endowment. There have been notorious cases of misuse of waqf funds, and government confiscation of waqf properties in order to control civil society. And ordinary citizens always had the right to appeal to the caliph if they felt the need. Special courts were maintained for this purpose, called *mazalim* courts. Staffed by representatives of the central government, the officials of these courts had full discretionary power. People could appeal the decision of a local official or court, or lodge a criminal complaint, and the mazalim judge could make any decision he felt suitable, without being held accountable to standard Islamic law as established by the legal scholars. Theoretically, however, waqf endowments remain independent funds, allowing for the independence of legal scholars, who remain the arbiters of political legitimacy in the classic Islamic model.

Cultural Achievements

During the Middle Ages, Islam's unique system of religious freedom and administrative flexibility allowed for remarkable stability and growth. It also produced a period of peace and prosperity in which the sciences and arts were brought to new levels of perfection. The Islamic world from Spain to India – with its plurality of cultures, ethnicities, and religious communities – produced an unrivaled cultural efflorescence. At its root was an openness to diverse heritages and intellectual influences. The environment produced was one in which learning was both a cherished value and a collective pursuit. Muslim scholars who discovered long-forgotten Greek texts in Egyptian libraries worked with Christian scholars who could translate them into their native Syriac and then into Arabic. Combining them with the intellectual heritage of Persia and India, these scholars built a magnificent cultural edifice that included the most advanced science and arts of the age. As Dennis Overbye recently characterized it: "Commanded by the [Quran] to seek knowledge and read nature for signs of the Creator, and inspired by a treasure trove of ancient Greek learning, Muslims created a society that in the Middle Ages was the scientific center of the world. The Arabic language was synonymous with learning and science for 500 years, a golden age that can count among its credits the precursors to modern universities, algebra, the names of the stars and even the notion of science as an empirical inquiry."[8]

The Abbasid court of Harun al-Rashid (d. 809), immortalized in the stories of the *Thousand and One Nights*, is best known in the West for its splendor. The royal palace, surrounded by beautiful gardens, was so huge that its upkeep required hundreds of servants. It reputedly had thousands of finely woven carpets and curtains of spun gold. The queen's table was set only with dishes of gold and silver, inlaid with precious stones. The king's audience chamber was known as the Hall of the Tree, named after the decorative artificial tree that was its centerpiece; it was handmade of gold and silver and had mechanical golden birds chirping in its branches. Baghdad was undoubtedly the center of the civilized world. It received envoys from around the globe, including the court of Charlemagne, Harun al-Rashid's contemporary. (Harun also sent envoys to Charlemagne. In response to a request from Charlemagne, Harun sent as a gift to the court at Aachen a white elephant. Its name was Abu Abbas, meaning "Father of Abbas," in honor of the Abbasid caliphate. The elephant survived for eight years in the harsh European climate.) The wealth of Harun's court was based not only on taxes collected from the Abbasids' enormous holdings, but from trade in prized goods from Africa, India, China, Central Asia, Russia, and beyond. Coins minted there have been found as far north as Germany, Sweden, and Finland. Medieval Islamic Spain was at least as sophisticated as Baghdad. In the tenth century, Cordoba, the capital of Umayyad Spain, was known throughout Europe as a great city. Under Muslim rule, its population had nearly quadrupled to 100,000, roughly equivalent to the population of Constantinople at the time. Its streets were illuminated by thousands of state-maintained lanterns; it had hundreds of fountains and baths supplied by aqueducts. It enjoyed unprecedented prosperity based on an agricultural revolution that included the introduction of new irrigation techniques and crops. Oranges (the name comes from the Arabic, *naranj*) and lemons (from the Arabic, *limun*), artichokes (from the Persian and Arabic, *ardi shoki*), cotton (from the Arabic, *qutun*), and sugar cane (from the Arabic, *sukkar*) are among the many crops introduced to Europe at this time. The city also had public libraries. The court library alone had over 400,000 books. (The largest library in Europe at the time, in a Swiss monastery, held approximately 600 books.)

Indeed, although its political power would inevitably fade, intellectual achievements are the lasting legacy of the Islamic empire. Even before the time of Harun al-Rashid, translation of classical Hellenic texts had begun. These were texts that had lain in oblivion in Egyptian libraries after the decline of classical Greece, and included the medical works of Galen and Hippocrates, and Ptolemy's and Euclid's work on mathematics and astronomy. The value of the texts was immediately recognized in the Islamic world, and the work of translation was considered so important that a family of Christian translators, Hunayn b. Ishaq (d. 873) and his son and nephew, achieved widespread fame for their work. They improved on earlier translations and expanded the works available in Arabic to include those of Aristotle and Plato. According to legend, Harun's successor al-Mamun placed so much value on learning that he paid Hunayn the weight of the books he translated in gold.

Based on these translations, scholars in the Muslim world developed an intellectual culture unrivaled in the West since the days of classical Greece. Among the earliest areas to develop was the rational analysis of revealed truths. By adapting Greek rationalism to revelation, they developed Islamic philosophy. In doing so, their works became both sources for European knowledge of classical Greek learning, and models for developing

Christian and Judaic philosophies. Al-Farabi (Alpharabius, in Latin; d. 950), for example, from Turkic Central Asia, composed commentaries on Plato and Aristotle, as well as a description of the ideal Islamic state. For him, that was "The Virtuous City" (*al-madinat al-fadilah*), headed by a morally and intellectually enlightened leader for the benefit of its inhabitants. The two most influential philosophers in the Muslim world were Ibn Sina (Avicenna, in Latin; d. 1037) and Ibn Rushd (Averroes, in Latin; d. 1198). Ibn Sina, from Bukhara (in modern Uzbekistan), was perhaps the most broad-ranging intellect of the medieval Islamic world. He wrote on art, astronomy, geometry, and medicine, among other topics. But his most lasting influence – even to the modern age – is in philosophy. His rational clarification of Islamic teaching was heavily influenced by his reading of Plato and Aristotle, and established the model for medieval philosophical

Plate 1   Raphael's *School of Athens* showing Ibn Rushd with Aristotle. Photo AKG Images/Pirozzi.

theology. Ibn Rushd of Cordoba (Spain) more accurately interpreted Aristotelian thought, and became early medieval Europe's most important source of knowledge of Aristotle.

The Muslims' work was controversial both in the Muslim world and beyond. Rational articulation of religious principles given in revelation, if kept within the limits of revelation, was acceptable to traditional scholars. That is what we call theology (called *kalam*, in Arabic; see Chapter 4 for a further discussion of kalam). But philosophy had no theoretical limits to its rational inquiry. In cases in which the results of rational inquiry seemed to conflict with revelation, philosophers generally concluded that revelation should be understood as metaphor for deeper truths inaccessible to the untrained mind. Such conclusions were unacceptable to religious scholars. This controversy prompted one of the most interesting philosophical exchanges of the medieval world: theologian al-Ghazali's (d. 1111) critique of philosophers for "incoherence" (*Tahafut al-falasifa*, The Incoherence of the Philosophers), and philosopher Ibn Rushd's response (*Tahafut al-tahafut*, The Incoherence of Incoherence).

Al-Ghazali was a Persian scholar of law, philosophy, and theology, but he experienced a spiritual crisis at the height of his intellectual career and turned to mysticism. There he found spiritual sustenance and became convinced that the practices of Sufism (see "Spirituality," below) were the only source of the kind of certainty necessary to sustain a life of faith. That is what motivated him to write his diatribe against philosophers' attempts to find certainty through reason. He attempted to show that logical analysis was inherently incapable of dealing with religious truth and inevitably led to self-contradiction. Among his arguments was that if logic were capable of bringing certainty on metaphysical issues, then everyone would agree on them, just as everyone agrees on the conclusions of logic regarding mathematics, for example. But, in fact, philosophers disagree all the time about these issues. Al-Ghazali attacked a number of specific philosophical arguments, but was most concerned with proofs for the existence of God, since they entailed the claim that the universe is eternal, rather than created in time. Some philosophers had made use of Aristotle's argument about the need for a "prime mover" – a force to originate all motion, change, and causality in the universe – to prove that there must be a God, an "unmoved mover." The Prime Mover, as God, was eternal and perfect, and that means that the Prime Mover is also changeless, since change implies going from a state of incompleteness (or "potentiality," in philosophical language) to completeness ("actuality," in philosophical language). Therefore, the universe must also be eternal, or else one would have to claim that God changed (or moved) when He decided at some point to create the world. Because this conclusion contradicts the revealed truth of creation, al-Ghazali tried to demonstrate its fallacy. He said the problem was that the philosophers had failed to distinguish between the originator of the action and the action itself. He concluded that God willed from all eternity that the world and everything in it would eventually be created. But that does not mean that the created things themselves are eternal. In response, Ibn Rushd pointed out that al-Ghazali had failed to distinguish between willing something and actually doing it. One can decide to do something long before one does it, but it will not be done until the person who made the decision adds action to decision, bringing us right back to where we started: either the world is eternal or God is not perfect. Neither side was convinced by the other's arguments, and the theologians and philosophers parted ways.

In Europe, as well, Ibn Rushd inspired a school of thought known as Latin Averroism that vied with Thomas Aquinas' scholastic theology, which itself was based on the understanding of Aristotle that he had derived from the Muslim philosophers. This controversy prompted Aquinas to pen one of his more famous works, *Summa contra gentiles*, attempting to refute the beliefs of the "heathen" Muslims. It also landed Ibn Rushd/Averroes in Dante's lowest level of hell.

Jewish thinkers in the Muslim world also attempted to rationalize revealed religion by means of ancient Greek philosophy. Working with texts that typically were translated from Greek into Syriac into Arabic and then into Hebrew, Jewish thinkers followed the same patterns as their Muslim compatriots. Ben Gabirol's (d. *ca.* 1058) *Yanbu' al-hayah* (The Fount of Life) was an important source of Platonic thought in Islamic Spain as well as in Europe. The great Mosheh ben Maymon of Cordoba (d. 1204; Maimonides, in Latin; Musa ibn Maymon, in Arabic) was both a distinguished philosopher and physician, highly placed in the royal court. He was the personal physician to Salah al-Din (Saladdin, of Crusades fame; see Chapter 3).

Although highly respected in the Islamic world as in Europe, philosophy was relatively marginal to the daily life of medieval society. Of more obvious benefit were the practical sciences on which medieval Islam's advanced civilization was based. And of the practical sciences, the most prized was medicine. Al-Ghazali even counted the study of medicine as a religious duty, incumbent on a sufficient number of Muslims to meet the needs of the community. Medical expertise was so highly valued that, according to tradition, it was first revealed by God (through the prophet Idris/Enoch). Scholars in the Muslim world developed the most advanced medical research of the age. The Abbasids were particularly interested in supporting medical research. Harun al-Rashid established the first hospital in Baghdad under the guidance of Christian scholars trained at Gundaishapur Hospital, a research institute established in sixth-century Persia (Iran). By the end of the ninth century several other hospitals had been established in Cairo, Mecca, and Medina, as well, and mobile medical units established for rural areas. These hospitals treated males and females, had outpatient facilities, and offered services for the poor. Many of the hospitals had mental wards, libraries, and classrooms. By the early tenth century, standard exams were needed in order to practice medicine in Baghdad, a city with nearly nine hundred registered physicians. The Mansuri hospital in Cairo, built in the thirteenth century, is still in use today for the treatment of the blind. It had a policy of turning away no one, regardless of gender, religion, or financial means, and was equipped with specialty wards, a pharmacy, lecture rooms, a library, and a chapel as well as a mosque. By the fourteenth century, a number of hospitals had been established in Islamic India as well. As in the Arab world, medical treatment was free, supported by waqf endowments and government patronage.

The famous Persian medical researcher al-Razi (d. 925) worked at an institute in Baghdad that had twenty-four doctors, each with a different specialization. His *Kitab al-asrar* (Book of Secrets), translated into Latin in the twelfth century (De spiritibus et corporibus), was a foundational text on alchemy, the forerunner to modern chemistry. His compilations of medical knowledge were likewise translated into Latin and remained standard sources in Europe as late as the sixteenth century. Even more influential was the philosopher-physician Ibn Sina. Not only were his commentaries on Aristotle a primary source for Latin scholars, but his compendium of Greek and Islamic medical knowledge – *al-Qanun fi'l-tibb* – was an authoritative text for European scholars. It was unsurpassed by Western scholars for 600 years.

Diseases of the eye were common in the Middle Eastern and North African climate of intense sun, sand, and dust. As a result, ophthalmology was among the medical specialties in which Islamic scholars made significant advances. The oldest existing systematic treatment of the subject is that of Christian scholar Ibn Masawayh from the ninth century. Trained as a mathematician, Ibn al-Haytham (b. 965) was inspired by Ptolemy's work on optics and made significant contributions to the understanding of vision. He developed a theory of vision incorporating Aristotelian ideas of matter and form with careful observations of anatomical experiments. In the process, he advanced the development of scientific method. His *Kitab al-manzir* (Book of Optics) includes as well important descriptions of reflections and refraction.

Also associated with practical needs were technical developments, including those in the field of optics. Technicians produced magnifying and refracting lenses that aided in both microscopic and macroscopic viewing. Navigational instruments such as the astrolabe and sextant were perfected and produced in abundance. But perhaps the most universally useful technological development was the introduction of the use of paper, in the late 700s, replacing parchment (the skin of sheep or goats) as the preferred writing surface. The use of paper was introduced in the eastern Islamic empire from China. Its use spread quickly westward. In Islamic Spain writing paper was produced locally. It was via Spain that the use of paper was introduced to Europe, although its use was limited until the Europeans developed moveable type.

Mathematics was a basic field in the medieval Muslim world and another area in which Muslim scholars excelled, again for very practical purposes. Accurate calculations were essential for efficient navigation, and the numerical system dominant in the ancient world simply did not allow the kind of accuracy these calculations demanded. Perhaps the most important contribution made in this area was Arabic numerals, replacing the letters used in Greek and Roman letter-based systems. These numbers – which in Arabic are called *hindi*, since they were originally Indian – were adapted for use, along with the zero (*sifr*, in Arabic; in English, cipher), in advanced calculations by al-Khwarizmi in the ninth century. Translated into Latin in the twelfth century, al-Khwarizmi's work was the source of the West's knowledge of algebra (*al-jabr*, which he developed in his book *Hisab al-jabr wa'l-muqabalah* [Calculation of Integration and Equation]). Al-Khwarizmi's work was also the source of the term algorithm, a Latin transliteration of al-Khawarizmi's name. Around the same time, al-Battani developed trigonometry. Like other mathematicians in the Islamic world, al-Battani studied the classical texts, verifying and refining their work and correcting some of Ptolemy's calculations of the lunar and planet orbits.

Al-Biruni (d. 1048) was a prolific scholar and scientist, working in the eastern cultural center of Ghaznah (now Ghazni, in modern Afghanistan). Knowledgeable in Persian, Arabic, Hebrew, Turkish, Syriac, and Sanskrit, al-Biruni wrote treatises on mathematics, astronomy, and ancient calendars, among other things. He supported the theory of the rotation of the earth, conceived to be a sphere, against those who argued that the world was flat. He also accurately calculated the longitudes and latitudes of the earth. At the other end of the Islamic empire, the Spanish mathematician and astronomer al-Zarqali (d. *ca.* 1087) made numerous profound discoveries concerning the movement of the stars and perfected the astrolabe in the process. The science of astronomy was so highly developed in the Islamic world that permanent observatories were established. The ruins of what is probably the oldest observatory in the world are still visible in Maragheh, in northwestern Iran. Built in 1259, it attracted scholars from as far away as China, and included an extensive library. The contributions of astronomers from medieval Islam were also immortalized in the names they gave to various stars, such as Altair (*al-tair*, the flyer) and Betelgeuse (*bayt al-Jawzi*, the home of Jawzi, the Arabic name for Orion), as well as technical terms like zenith (*as-samt*) and nadir (*nadhir*).

The translations of classical Greek, Persian, and Indian texts, in the intellectually charged atmosphere of medieval Islam, became the basis of the Muslim world's great cultural flowering in the Middle Ages. They were the basis of Europe's, as well, transmitted to Europe via Syria, Sicily, and especially Spain. A school was established in eleventh-century Toledo specifically for translating Arabic texts into Latin, the language of learning throughout Europe. There scholars came from as far away as England and Scotland to discover the learning of the Islamic empire and transmit it to Europe. The first translation of the Quran was produced at this school by Robert of Chester and Herman the Dalmatian at the request of Peter the Venerable, the abbot of Cluny in France. It was also in Toledo that the classics of Hellenic learning were translated from Arabic into Latin. The debt of Europe to the medieval Islamic scholars is impossible to measure. As historian Philip Hitti put it, "[H]ad the researches of Aristotle, Galen and Ptolemy been lost to posterity the world would have been as poor as if they had never been produced."[9]

Spirituality

Preserving, developing, and passing on classical studies was not the only contribution of the medieval Muslim world to global culture. Islamic scholars also produced wholly original works, laying the foundations for academic disciplines that were not developed in the Western world until the modern era. The work of Ibn Khaldun (d. 1406) is a case in point. His *Muqaddimah* (Introduction [to the History of the Arabs, Persians, and Berbers]) is often cited as the first work of historiography and forerunner to the modern studies of anthropology, sociology, economics, and political science. In it he outlines patterns of social and political development, observing along the way patterns in history and economics. That is why historian Arnold Toynbee declared the *Mudqaddimah* to be "the greatest work of its kind that has ever yet been created by any mind."[10] Ibn Khaldun was often quoted by US President Ronald Reagan, in fact, on the relationship between tax cuts and inflation.[11] He clearly predicted the observations of Marx concerning the impact of historical conditions on human development. In order to understand social, political, and historical developments, he said, we must understand political principles, how the peoples in question make their livings, their level of education, their religious beliefs and customs, whether they live in rural or urban conditions, and how they govern themselves. His insistence that individual events be understood in terms of their causes, since nothing occurs in a vacuum, became an essential principle of modern historiography.

Ibn Khaldun was also an advocate of critical thinking. He rebuked scholars who simply transmit received wisdom without examining it in light of new information, and those who write with political bias, "smearing the reputation of others" for the sake of "selfish interests and rivalries, or swayed by vendors of tyranny and dishonesty."[12] Ibn Khaldun was fond of quoting Prophet Muhammad's assertion that "scholars are the heirs of the prophets," and perhaps no individual scholar or sentiment better captures the vibrant intellectual spirit of the medieval Muslim world than this brilliant and multifaceted scholar.

But there was another side to medieval Islam, besides the sophisticated bureaucracies and highly public, creative scholarship. The inward, personal side of Islam was also developing into a deeply spiritual tradition known as Sufism. For all the great achievements of Islamic rulers and scholars, Islam remains essentially a personal commitment. Law deals with the external manifestation of believers' personal commitment. Muslims believe that sincere belief will be manifested outwardly in righteous actions. But the core of those actions is still internal. Pious actions reflect a kind of turning of the will that is at once passive and active. It is a giving of oneself to the divine will, but in so doing, it is also a commitment to do the things necessary to achieve the divine will. This unique combination of acceptance and commitment – this *islam* – is expressed in the Quran as the virtue *taqwa*. The Quran calls for faith, hope, and charity – the virtues most commonly discussed in Christianity – in terms that are directly parallel to their English meanings (*iman, amal, sadaqa*). But *taqwa* is not easy to translate. As discussed in Chapter 1, its common translation as "fear of God" is misleading. The term comes from a root that has to do with protection, preservation, or security. Even the Quran never defines the term, in the sense of limiting it to some specific action or actions. Instead, as noted, it gives examples of the kind of behavior that stems from a well-formed conscience. For example, the Quran tells people not to allow other people's unjust actions to lead them to unfair behavior. "So long as [the polytheists] stay true to you, stay true to them. Indeed, God loves those with taqwa." (9:7) Taqwa does involve virtuous behavior, but it is not just an external thing. Taqwa is also intentions. It is the internalization of God's will. Taqwa is the willing choice to allow one's conscience to be guided by God, expressed externally through goodness and charity. That willing submission to God will inevitably express itself through righteous behavior – and the combination will preserve the believer from real danger – the danger of eternal punishment.

But how does one develop such virtue? Scholars and lawyers can help guide understanding and actions. But making God's will your own requires spiritual practice. This inward, spiritual aspect of Islamic practice, Sufism, is often called "interior Islam." It can also be described as mature Islam. Whereas a child is motivated to do good and avoid evil based on the promise of reward and the threat of punishment, a mature believer takes personal gratification in virtuous deeds and finds evil deeds personally repugnant. Sufi teachings and practice grew in Islam as a way to help people develop this ability to find joy in virtue.

Sufism has roots in the earliest centuries of Islam. During the lifetime of Prophet Muhammad, the community benefited not only from religious and political leadership, but also from his personal example. The Prophet lived a life fully motivated by the desire to do the will of God. He did warn people that there was a difference between those of his choices that were inspired by God and those that were simply based on his best judgment. For example, when people asked him questions about planting their crops, he reminded them that he knew no more about it than they did. What is more, the Quran instructs Muhammad to consult with his community concerning decisions that affect them, establishing a basis for democracy in Islam according to many modern interpreters. Nevertheless, the Quran tells people that Muhammad sets the best example of Islamic behavior. His personal choices, the way he conducted his life and treated people all served as examples that inspired his community to piety. But his death left a void in this regard. As the scholars and other officials established the details of Islamic institutions, the challenge of providing spiritual guidance was taken up by individuals – some scholarly, some not – who simply gained reputations in the community for their ability to inspire and lead others to righteousness.

Among the most effective ways to inspire piety was through stories about the Prophet and his family. Some people became extremely popular for their ability to move audiences with stories of the Prophet's virtue and wisdom, attracting audiences of spiritual seekers from far and wide. The most effective of these people attracted followers who stayed with them in order to further develop their spirituality. Gradually, centers of spiritual practice began to appear throughout the Muslim world. People would gather in the evenings for extra instruction and prayer sessions. Many such sessions incorporated practices designed to enhance spiritual awareness, such as rhythmic chanting of phrases or verses from the Quran. These spiritual "concerts" or *dhikr* sessions characterize much of Sufi practice today.

One of the earliest of the inspiring spiritual guides was a young woman from Iraq named Rabia (d. 801). According to legend, she was born into poverty and sold into slavery. But her piety so inspired her owners that she was freed, so that she could inspire others to lives of utter devotion and absolute, selfless love of God. Numerous verses, attributed to her and passed down through the ages, still have the ability to inspire. She confesses to God, for example, that she has two kinds of love for Him. She does nothing but think of God all day, but she says that is a selfish kind of love because it brings her so much happiness. The love that God deserves, she says, is one that strips away all separation between herself and God, so that she is no longer even aware of herself. Elsewhere, Rabia asks God to let her burn in hell if her devotion is motivated by fear of hell, and keep her out of heaven if she is only motivated by hope of reward. Her goal – and that of many Sufis – is to love God without external motivation. The teaching of the scholars is important, but it is only a first step toward spiritual awareness, in the Sufi view. As Rabia puts it, "The real work is in the Heart."[13]

Rabia was followed by countless others. Eventually, various "ways" or "paths" (tariqas, often translated as "orders") toward spiritual goals developed around the most successful spiritual guides. One of the most popular Sufi orders remains the Qadiri, named after Abd al-Qadir al-Gilani (d. 1166), the person who inspired its founders. As a youth al-Gilani went to Baghdad to study religion and became an expert in philosophy and law. But he became known for his inspiring sermons advising Muslims how to go beyond mere obedience to fully spiritual religious practice. Some popular preachers focused on the need for self-discipline and even asceticism (avoiding all but the bare necessities of life, including fasting and sexual abstinence). These were the people, in fact, who gave Sufism its name. The term "sufi" comes from the word *suf* (wool), signifying the simple, coarse clothing worn by many spiritual seekers. But al-Gilani stressed charity, honesty, and sincerity – all virtues that are distinctly social in outlook. His own life was a model of the kind of spiritual search that leads people to Sufism. A story is told, for example, of his trip to Baghdad as a young student. His mother had sewn his money into the lining of his clothes so that he would not lose it on the trip. But on the trip his caravan was waylaid by robbers. The thieves demanded that everyone give them their money and jewels, but they overlooked the ragged-looking boy. When he realized what was happening, al-Gilani told the robbers that he had some money, too. The criminals were so moved by the boy's honesty and sincerity that they converted on the spot and went on to live virtuous lives.

As with many spiritual leaders, stories about the power of al-Gilani's piety spread quickly. The Qadiri order and its offshoots spread throughout the Middle East, westward across North Africa and eastward to China and South Asia. Unlike some orders that devised their own sets of rules, Qadiris were advised to simply follow Islamic legal codes and internalize them through spiritual practice. The Qadiri order was also relatively informal, unlike some orders that required strict initiation rites and distinctive practices, and flexible so that local customs in various regions could be accommodated. It remains among the most widespread orders in the world today. Al-Gilani's tomb in Baghdad is still a popular pilgrimage site.

Other orders are perhaps better known in the West, such as the Mevlevis or "Whirling Dervishes." The Mevlevis incorporate a rhythmic spinning into their prayer recitals. The spinning motion makes their full white robes fan out in a dramatic display. That spectacle, accompanied by music, is a popular feature at Spiritual recitals worldwide, and even earned the Mevlevis an invitation to perform at Carnegie Hall. The founder of their order, Jalal al-Din Rumi (d. 1273), is also well known in the

Plate 2   Mevlevis or "Whirling dervishes." © Ian Berry/Magnum.

West. His exquisite poetry is among the best-selling poetry in America today, indicating the broad appeal of the basic spirituality underlying Islamic practice. Rumi, originally from Afghanistan but brought up in Byzantine Turkey, was a scholar and teacher until his spiritual awakening in middle age. His poetry beautifully expresses the yearning for spiritual freedom that characterizes much of Sufism. It is a desire to be released from the bonds of selfishness, desire, and greed, to be completely absorbed in divine goodness and beauty. Like Rabia, Rumi encourages people to go beyond the externals of religious practice, and seek deeper personal awareness:

> For years, copying other people, I tried to know myself.
> From within, I couldn't decide what to do.
> Unable to see, I heard my name being called.
> Then I walked outside.

The key to spiritual awareness, he says, will not be found in books:

> Today, like every other day, we wake up empty
> and frightened. Don't open the door to the study
> and begin reading. Take down a musical instrument.
> Let the beauty we love be what we do.
> There are hundreds of ways to kneel and kiss the ground.[14]

Sufism was challenging for the religious authorities, of course. The new spiritual leaders seemed to challenge the authority of the legal scholars and theologians, especially by holding prayer sessions independent of the mosque and establishing rules separate from Islamic legal codes. Furthermore, some of the Sufis' ecstatic expressions of spiritual joy seemed downright blasphemous. For example, the tenth-century Persian al-Hallaj expressed his sense of being spiritually fulfilled by proclaiming, "I am the Truth." Unfortunately for him, this claim was taken to be equivalent to saying, "I am God," since "the Truth" is one of the divine names. Al-Hallaj was famously martyred in Baghdad and thrown into the Tigris River. When Sufi scholars tried to explain their positions philosophically, they likewise ran into trouble. The famous Spanish mystic Ibn al-Arabi (d. 1240), for example, explained that the goal of the religious seeker is reunion with God, the source of all being. For him, all being is ultimately one in God anyway. But claims like that seem to blur the distinction between the Creator and creatures, so Ibn al-Arabi's "philosophy of illumination" was condemned by many orthodox theologians. (See Chapter 4 for further discussion of Sufism.)

Nevertheless, Islamic mysticism, from its simple piety to its complex philosophy, was ultimately accepted as an integral part of Islamic tradition. The desire for personal religious experiences could not be legislated away. Al-Ghazali is usually given credit for having confirmed the value of mysticism through his works demonstrating the limitations of reason and law in developing true spirituality. Even such a public person as Ibn Khaldun – who was not only a scholar but also held numerous important government positions throughout his life – periodically took refuge at Sufi lodges to contemplate and write. Today there are hundreds of Sufi orders spread throughout the Muslim world, including the United States.

Conclusion

The extraordinary accomplishments of the medieval Muslim world stand as a tribute to the dynamism and creativity in the service of humanity that many see as the true spirit of Islam. Many Muslims see them as a reflection of the Quran's unique commitment to intellectual endeavor. The Quran commands even Prophet Muhammad to seek knowledge (20:114). But as Ibn Khaldun observed, no empire lasts forever. Muslims soon faced the challenges of epidemic disease, internal conflict, and external attacks that would eventually shake the empire to its very core. But the law, science, and spirituality developed in the medieval world would survive, and serve as a foundation for reorganization and renewed growth in the Muslim world, until it was ultimately subdued by European colonization.

Chapter 3

Division and Reorganization

The Crusades and Other Disasters

Among the catastrophes that struck the Muslim world in the late Middle Ages was the Black Death. That was the name given to the bubonic plague, a gruesome, deadly disease that swept Europe in the mid-fourteenth century, killing up to two thirds of the population in some places. In England alone it reduced the population by half. But the plague hit the Muslim world equally hard. From the Black Sea, trading ships spread it throughout the Mediterranean, including Islamic North Africa and Spain, killing more than half the population in some cities.

Unfortunately, the plague was not the only disaster to hit the medieval Muslim world. They were also besieged by European invaders fighting a holy war for Christianity. By the tenth century, Europe had become mired in corruption and conflict. Much of it stemmed from the competition for supreme power between the Holy Roman emperors and the popes. This was not a struggle between secular and sacred, or earthly and heavenly authority. The competitors did not believe they were in the process of dividing up spheres of influence (even though that

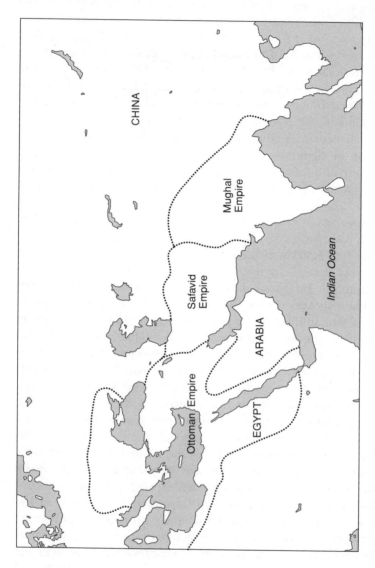

Map 2 Muslim world in the sixteenth century.

is how it turned out in the long run). Both the emperors and the popes struggled for overall authority on earth, sanctioned by heaven. At the end of the eleventh century, Pope Urban II was determined to reassert church leadership, not just in the spiritual realm but the earthly as well. A request from the Byzantine emperor in Constantinople (in modern Turkey) for assistance in his struggle against the growing power of the Muslims in the Middle East provided the perfect opportunity. The chance for Rome to help Constantinople had the added bonus of demonstrating that the pope was leader of both Western and Eastern Christians. Pope Urban II therefore called a Church council and challenged his Christian warriors to rise to the occasion.

Christians were already prone to be suspicious of Muslims. They had heard that they were "infidels," followers of a "false prophet." St. John of Damascus (d. 749) had described Islam as a heresy derived from Christian sources.[1] Eulogius, the Bishop of Cordoba during the ninth century, when Cordoba was the capital of Islamic Spain, did not help matters. He claimed that when Muhammad died, Muslims expected angels to come and take him to heaven. Instead, he said, dogs consumed his body and therefore Muslims conduct an annual slaughter of dogs. Clearly, fear of Muslims was growing in Christian Europe. By the end of the tenth century, the story of a minor battle between Charlemagne and the Basques at Roncesvalles in the eighth century had been transformed into one of France's earliest epics, the "Song of Roland." In this telling of the story, Charlemagne's enemies were not the Basques but the Muslims of Spain. The Muslims, so the story goes, had colluded with a disgruntled French soldier and killed one of France's noblest knights. The poem was the source of another version of the story of Muhammad's death, this one with pigs consuming the Prophet's body. This story was used to explain the Muslim prohibition of the consumption of pork. Other interpretations explain that Muhammad was killed by the pigs while he was drunk and

that, Christian audiences were told, was why Muslims also prohibit drinking alcoholic beverages.[2]

According to the increasing rumors in Europe about Muslims,
not only were they infidels, but they were ruthless killers determined to take over the world. They had already taken over
most of Spain, along with parts of southern France and Sicily,
not to mention the formerly Christian Byzantine lands in the
Middle East – including the "Holy Land." Such stories prepared
the ground for the papal call to arms, issued in 1095. Pope Urban
II is reported to have contributed to the fear of Muslims as
he tried to encourage his faithful at the Council of Clermont to
join in his holy war. His stories of hideous torture of Christians,
including brutal circumcisions, aroused terror and hatred, of
course. But vengeance was hardly a Christian virtue, and killing
was still considered a mortal sin. It was a violation of both a
sacred commandment and the example set by Jesus Christ. Since
the fourth century, when Christianity had become politicized
under the emperor Constantine, Christians had been called upon
to serve as soldiers, but they still had to do penance if they killed
someone. But with the Crusades came the transformation of
Christianity from a pacifist religion to one that fully condoned
war under certain circumstances. Pope Urban II told his flock
that killing people in wars declared just by the Church was not
a sin. It was virtuous, in fact, and any sincere fighter who died
in the process became a martyr. All punishment due in the
afterlife for sins committed in the here and now would be waived;
the martyr was assured immediate entry into heaven.

Thus, it became both a Christian duty and a quick route to
"present and eternal glory"[3] to join in the holy war against
Muslims, and many Europeans responded to the papal call
enthusiastically. Rich and poor, professional and amateur, European Christians joined the call to retake the Holy Land. Wave
after wave, they came into Muslim lands, killing Jews and Christians as well as the Muslims who were their main target. The
first army of Crusaders captured Antioch and Jerusalem, killing

all its inhabitants. They then established their own "Crusader states" in Jerusalem, Tripoli, Antioch, and Edessa. The second Crusade, called by Pope Eugenius III in 1144, failed in its effort to take Damascus. Eventually, Salah al-Din ("Saladin," d. 1193) succeeded in organizing the Muslims sufficiently to fight back against the European invaders. An Iraqi Kurd who served the Muslim ruling family in Syria and Egypt, he led the campaign to recapture Jerusalem in 1187. The Europeans continued their invasions periodically over the next two centuries. But their last stronghold in the area, Tripoli, was retaken by Muslims in 1289. The ruins of Crusader castles remain in the Middle East, as does the chilling effect of the term "crusade." It recalls the brutality of the Christians and the contempt they showed for anyone who did not share their European Christian identity.

To this day, the treachery of the European invaders is recalled with horror. When the Muslims conquered Jerusalem from the Byzantines in 638, Caliph Umar guaranteed the security of its Christian inhabitants, their property and churches. When the European Christians took Jerusalem in 1099, according to their own accounts, their leaders promised security to those who surrendered. But, except for a few men who had barricaded themselves in a tower, the Christian soldiers slaughtered all the inhabitants, men, women, and children, Muslim and Jewish. Then the Europeans disemboweled the corpses, to get at the gold coins they believed the Muslims had "gulped down their loathsome throats."[4] In Jerusalem's al-Aqsa mosque alone, according to Muslim sources, the crusaders killed "more than 70,000 people, among them a large number of imams and Muslim scholars, devout and ascetic men who had left their homelands to live lives of pious seclusion in the Holy Place."[5]

Although these figures are probably exaggerated, the plight of the victims of the European Crusaders was no doubt dire, and was known throughout the Arab Muslim world. One of the historians at the time, Ibn al-Athir (d. 1234), quotes the lament of an Iraqi poet of the era:

> We have mingled blood with flowing tears, and there is not
> room left in us for pity.
> To shed tears is a man's worst weapon when the swords stir
> up the embers of war.
> Sons of Islam, behind you are battles in which heads rolled
> at your feet.
> Dare you slumber in the blessed shade of safety, where life
> is as soft as an orchard flower?
> How can the eye sleep between the lids at a time of disasters
> that would waken any sleeper?[6]

Despite the sympathy for the Crusaders' victims, and the strong desire to rescue them, Muslims are proud to recall the valor and restraint shown by Salah al-Din as he rescued Jerusalem, in contrast with the Crusaders' butchery. It took nearly a century for the Muslims to regain Jerusalem, but eventually the European leaders surrendered the city and asked for general amnesty for all its inhabitants. Otherwise, they said they would kill all their wives, children, prisoners and animals, and destroy the Islamic holy places. Salah al-Din granted them amnesty and allowed them to be ransomed by their people. Even though the Christian leader of Jerusalem looted both the Christian and Islamic holy sites, Salah al-Din let him go and had him escorted to Tyre. The Muslims were horrified that the ancient holy site, al-Aqsa mosque, had been used by the Christians as a storeroom and latrine, yet Salah al-Din did not rescind his amnesty. He simply ordered the shrines cleansed and restored to their original use.

In fact, Salah al-Din was not always so magnanimous. There is a horrific eyewitness account of the treatment received by two groups of religious warriors – the Templars and the Hospitallers, who had terrorized Muslims for years. Salah al-Din had some 200 of them beheaded, and the onlooker who gives us the gory report claims that the soldiers who carried out the executions received great praise. This was a violation of Islamic norms which forbid killing prisoners of war. Obviously, Salah al-Din believed that even as prisoners these soldiers were a threat to the survival of the community; he treated the other captive knights with dignity and allowed them to be ransomed later. But most Muslims are unaware of this deviation from Salah al-Din's standard policies. To this day, in recognition of his nobility in victory at Jerusalem, Salah al-Din is eulogized as a model of Islamic virtue: "just, benign, merciful, quick to help the weak against the strong." He was generous, courageous, steadfast, humane, and forgiving.[7] Salah al-Din's valor and nobility had saved Islam from the Western invaders. Their subsequent campaigns – and there were many – were ultimately failures.

A third disaster then struck at the heart of the Muslim world. No sooner had the European invaders been vanquished than the Muslims were attacked from the other direction. Beginning in 1220, waves of Turkic tribesmen, called Mongols, came riding in from Central Asia, conquering everything in their path. Led by Genghis Khan, these nomads had no regard for settled, urban

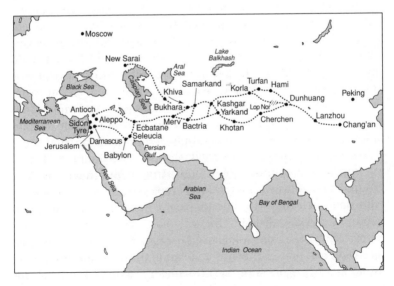

Map 3 The Silk Road.

life. But they did depend upon some of the products of the civilized populations of Islam's great trading cities along the Silk Road, and these became desirable targets for the mighty Mongols.

The Silk Road, made famous by Marco Polo in the thirteenth century, was the ancient trade route established in Greek and Roman times across the Middle East to China. It stretched from the Mediterranean to the Great Wall, crossing Syria, Persia, Afghanistan, Pakistan, India, and Central Asia. Along the route travelers had to contend with treacherous deserts and mountains, including the highest in the world – the Himalayas, the Hindu Kush, and Karakorum; excruciating heat and sub-zero temperatures; and bandits of every variety. Yet trade along the route thrived until sea travel was developed enough to make it more efficient than land travel over great distances. The silk traded by the Chinese gave the route its name, but it was not the only commodity of value for the thousands who engaged in Silk Road commerce. Precious metals, ivory, oils, skins, ceramics, glass, and spices were some of the other desired products. As well, explorers, missionaries, and conquerors used the route on their adventures. Afghanistan and what is now Pakistan were at the crossroads of the various trails that made up the Silk Road. Alexander the Great traveled to this region in the fourth century BCE. To this day, residents of the Hunza valley in Afghanistan claim to be descendants of Alexander's troops. Buddhists from India came into the region in the first century CE, establishing their religion and leaving the magnificent sculptures at Bamiyan that were destroyed by the Taliban in 2000. Nestorian Christians fled eastward from Roman authorities who had declared them heretical, in the fifth century, and two centuries later, Muslim traders and teachers along the Silk Road brought Islam as far as China, where it remains strong today.

The Silk Road was for centuries the most important bridge between the East and West. Along its route were some of the most magnificent cities of the ancient world. Bukhara, for example, in present-day Uzbekistan, was established at the site of an oasis by the first century CE. Built around a central fortress, the city provided both protection from the dangers of the road and a trading site. Its inhabitants' gold embroidery and metal-work were valuable commodities in the East–West trade. In the early eighth century, it was conquered by Arab Muslims and became a regional capital known for its beautiful mosques and many schools. One of the two leading hadith collectors, in fact, Abu 'Abd Allah Muhammad ibn Ismail (d. 870), was from there, which is why most people know him only as al-Bukhari. But Bukhara was attacked and destroyed by the Mongols, under Genghis Khan, in 1220, and twice thereafter in the next century. Ibn Battuta, the Islamic Marco Polo, visited the city in the 1330s and said, "Its mosques, colleges, and bazaars are in ruins . . . There is not one person in it today who possesses any religious learning or who shows any concern for acquiring it."[8] Samarkand, also in present-day Uzbekistan, was another ancient city of Central Asia. Originally called Maracanda, Samarkand was established at the crossroads of the India and China routes on the Silk Road. Alexander the Great captured it in 329 B.C.E. When it was conquered by Muslims in 711, the city was renamed Samarkand and remained an important and prosperous regional center. Bukhara and Samarkand were considered among the most beautiful cities in the Muslim world, but like Bukhara, Samarkand was also destroyed by Genghis Khan (1221).

Under Genghis Khan's successors, the Mongols continued their advance through the Muslim world. In 1258 they reached Baghdad and burned it to the ground. Unlike other Islamic centers like Mecca, Jerusalem, and Damascus, Baghdad was not an ancient city. It was a planned city, established on the banks of the Tigris River on the site of a Persian village in 762, as the Abbasid capital. Its architects set up Baghdad around the caliph's palace and a great mosque, with three concentric walls surrounding it and four roads leading out from the center to the four corners of the empire. Markets and suburbs were built outside the walls. Nicknamed Madinat al-Salam (City of Peace),

Baghdad quickly became the center of the empire's economic and cultural life. It was described in *The Thousand and One Nights* as one of the world's treasures. Ships from around the Indian Ocean and as far away as China visited its harbor. The city had known conflict in the years following the reign of Harun al-Rashid, but it was still thriving when Hulegu Khan, Genghis's grandson, and his troops descended upon it.

Some of the cities destroyed by the Mongols did recover. In Baghdad, the old Abbasid palace survives, as does the Mustansiriyyah, a school of higher Islamic learning built in 1234, but the city never regained its greatness until the modern era. Timur Lang, or Timur the Lame (Tamerlane, d. 1370), inherited the conquests of the Mongols. A Muslim born of Turkic parents near Samarkand, he took it upon himself to make Samarkand the most splendid capital of a reconstituted Mongol empire. He brought in experts to build great mosques and schools. His buildings were typically large, with domes and arched doorways, and decorated with marble and mosaics, many with gold and precious stones. They are still among the greatest architectural monuments of the Islamic world.

The Mongol invasions traditionally mark the end of the political unity of Islam. They also marked, for all practical purposes, the end of the Abbasid caliphate. While Baghdad burned, the Abbasid caliph packed up and moved to Cairo. His successors continued to be recognized as Islamic leaders, if in name only, until the last one was taken by Ottoman conquerors to Turkey in 1517. However, many areas of the Muslim world reorganized eventually and went on to great power and prestige. We will examine the rise of three of them: the Ottoman Turkish and Arab world, Safavid Iran, and Mughal India.

Decline of the Abbasids and Rise of the Ottomans

Egypt had already become autonomous. It was always difficult for the Islamic leaders to control Egypt from their capitals in

Medina, Damascus, and Baghdad. Rebellions in Egypt had marred the reign of the third caliph, Uthman, and there were sporadic uprisings against taxation and religious discrimination thereafter. By the ninth century, the caliphs had begun to grant tax revenues to people they appointed as administrators to this rich region. They also chose as administrators for these "tax farms" people with no tribal ties in the area, primarily Turks who had been purchased as slaves, in an effort to maintain loyalty to the central government alone. These Turkish administrators soon established themselves firmly enough to become independent, too, including setting up their own slave army. The architect of this independence was a governor named Ibn Tulun. Through careful management of agriculture and taxation, his administration grew rich and powerful, and was even able to take control of Syria from the caliph. He also built the famous Ibn Tulun mosque, still standing in Cairo. Ibn Tulun's son then extended Tulunid control to Iraq, as well. The Tulunids were overthrown by other foreign administrators, this time from Central Asia, who were then taken over by the Shii Fatimid dynasty (969–1171). The Fatimids took control of North Africa and significant portions of the Arabian peninsula.

The Fatimids (909–1171) were a formidable force. Their name comes from that of Prophet Muhammad's daughter Fatima, since they believe that only Muhammad's descendants through the marriage of his cousin Ali to his daughter Fatima were legitimate imams. Therefore, the Fatimids considered themselves not just independent of the Sunni Abbasid caliph, but the rightful holders of his title. From their original base in Yemen, they were able to establish sovereignty all across North Africa, as well as in Sicily, Syria, and western Arabia. They were fiercely committed to their cause, and gained the loyalty of many Muslims discontent with Abbasid rule. They quickly became wealthy and powerful. It was the Fatimids who established the city of Cairo in 969, and built it into a splendid center of military – including naval – power. Cairo was also a magnificent cultural center; the

Fatimids established al-Azhar University there, which was the first university in the Western world and is still thriving. But the Fatimids had their own problems with the question of succession. A group broke away from the rest of the Fatimids in 1094 when they believed the legitimate successor, Nizar, had been unfairly passed over in favor of his younger brother. Known in Islamic history as the Nizaris, this group plunged the regime into civil war. The group is known in European history as the Assassins, because they fought the Crusaders so fiercely. (The name "Assassins" comes from the Nizaris' alleged use of hashish to prepare themselves for battle; they were called the Hashishin "those who use Hashish").

The Fatimids were in power in Egypt when the Crusaders first descended upon Jerusalem. Many people believed that the Fatimids' lack of cooperation with Baghdad weakened the overall Muslim effort against the European Crusaders. They were the ones that Salah al-Din overthrew in order to return Egypt to the Sunni fold so that he could create a unified front against the Crusaders. But Salah al-Din also established an independent dynasty in Egypt, the Ayyubids (1171–1250). With the powerful army he established in Egypt he was able not only to defeat the Crusaders and gain control of Jerusalem and the Holy Land, but also to gain control over Syria, Iraq, Yemen, and western Arabia (Hijaz). Despite the stability and prosperity his victories brought to Egypt, power struggles developed. Like the Abbasids before them, the Ayyubids sought to maintain a loyal army by staffing it with slaves ("mamluks," from the Arabic term for "slave"), mainly Turkish. The idea was that as foreigners, these slaves would have no local loyalties that could develop into rival power structures. But by the end of the ninth century, mamluk soldiers had gained control of the Abbasid caliphate. Abbasids remained caliphs, but mamluks were the real rulers (sultans), and even they did not control the entire Muslim world. The caliph was acknowledged as the spiritual leader of the Muslim world but Egypt was autonomous. By the mid-thirteenth century, Ayyubid mamluks became Mamluks – in effect, their own dynasty in control of the Egyptian empire that Salah al-Din had established.

Not all Mamluk sultans placed their sons on the throne, but all were from a particular branch of former slave soldiers. And to ensure that they were recognized as legitimate rulers, the Mamluks invited the Abbasid caliph who had been deposed by the Mongols from his palace in Baghdad (1258) to take up residence in Cairo. By this time, there were no pretensions of combined religio-political rule. The caliph had no earthly power whatsoever. He was a symbol of Islamic unity, and gave legitimacy to the political rulers.

Making use of their own military, the Mamluks were effective rulers for the first half of their two-and-a-half-century reign. They became heroes by defeating the Sixth Crusade, and repulsed an early Mongol invasion (1260). But they were not able to fully protect their lands. By the fourteenth century, the plague had hit Egypt and decimated its population. What is more, the Europeans came back, this time not as warriors but as traders. Portuguese traders developed safe and efficient sea trade routes around the Indian Ocean, bypassing the overland routes that had been a significant source of revenue for the Mamluks. And the Mongols came back, too. After they had taken over the Abbasid capital in Baghdad, they established a number of regimes throughout Central and South Asia, and the Middle East.

By that time, the Mongols had become Muslims themselves, at least in name. The famous Timur Lang (Tamerlane), who would rebuild Samarkand and make it his splendid capital, tried to unify all the Mongols. He subdued the local khans (rulers) in Central Asia, the Crimea, Persia (which at that time included what is now western Afghanistan), and Mesopotamia (Iraq), and raided as far as Delhi in India. He was brutal beyond belief. Stories are told of entire cities' populations being massacred. His troops gained a reputation for being expert riders and archers who built towers of the skulls of their thousands of victims.

He was also successful, amassing the great wealth he used to rebuild and beautify Samarkand, for example. Inevitably, he turned again toward the Arab world. In 1401 he defeated Egypt's Mamluk army and took control of Syria and Iraq. Damascus was taken and Baghdad was once again destroyed.

By the time Timur died (in 1405, on his way to China), Mamluk power was on the wane. The Mamluks continued to rule Egypt, but they never recovered the country's economic prosperity or military might.

Another of the autonomous forces during Abbasid times with whom the Mongols tangled were the Seljuks (also spelled Seljuqs). The Seljuks were a dynasty named for the leader of one of the nomadic Turkic tribes from Central Asia. They began as border guards for a semi-autonomous Persian family (the Samanids; see below) in the ninth and tenth centuries. By the mid-eleventh century they were in control of Baghdad, ruling in the name of the Abbasid caliph.

The Ottomans were another Turkic dynasty. Like the Seljuks for whom they originally worked, they had begun as border warriors, guarding the northwest frontier against invasions and launching their own attacks against the Byzantine forces in the name of Islam. The power struggle between the Seljuks and Mongols weakened the Seljuks sufficiently to allow the Ottomans to firmly establish their power in Anatolia (present-day Turkey) in the thirteenth century. Their armies became a magnet for men seeking employment – both Muslims looking for work as *mujahiddin* (warriors in the struggle to spread Islam), and Christians looking for work as mercenaries. By the fourteenth century they had established a regular cavalry and an infantry – called the "new troops" or Janissaries, consisting mainly of converted Christian conscripts from the Balkans. By the end of that century, the Ottoman chief Bayezid had managed to establish sovereignty in the Balkans. The name of the Ottomans came to symbolize hope for a reunified Islamic empire; the nominal Abbasid caliphs in Cairo began to call the Ottomans sultans of

Islam, rather than the Mamluks under whose protection they were living.

By this time, the ferocious Timur Lang felt the challenge. Although he was busy expanding his sovereignty from Central Asia toward India, he decided to stop the advancing Ottoman powers. The two most powerful forces in the Islamic world at the time were competing for dominance. It was Timur's forces that triumphed in battle, at Ankara in 1402. But the result was not reunification of the empire. Timur's power would continue to be felt in the eastern regions, while the Ottomans continued their consolidation of power in the West.

The Europeans also began to worry about Ottoman expansion, and even organized a new Crusade (1444) to try to drive the Ottomans back across the Bosphorus (the straits that separate Europe from Asia). But it failed, largely because of the loyalty of the Serbian Christian rulers to the Ottoman sultan. In 1453, under Mehmed (Muhammad) II, "the Conqueror" (r. 1451–81), the Ottomans put an end to the Byzantine Empire, capturing Constantinople. Under its new name – Istanbul – it became the new Ottoman capital.

By the turn of the sixteenth century, Ottoman forces had subdued rival Muslim rulers in the region and expanded Ottoman sovereignty further in the Balkans – including Serbia, Bosnia, and Albania, as well as Crimea, and were well on their way to establishing naval superiority in the eastern Mediterranean. The idea of a reunified Islamic world may have been out of the question, but reunifying former Byzantine lands under the banner of the Ottoman sultan was not. The Ottomans just had to oust their Seljuk cousins from Syria and Egypt. That was accomplished by Sultan Selim II (r. 1512–20), who was just the man for the job. He had killed his own brothers and nephews, and four of his own five sons, to make sure no one interfered with his hold on the throne. By 1517 his forces had swept away the remaining impediments to Ottoman dominance in the Arab world, including the conquest of Syria and Egypt.

The way was thus clear for Selim's hand-picked – i.e., only surviving – successor, Suleiman, to become "the Lawgiver" (r. 1520–66). Suleiman's predecessors had established a stable administration. The practice of granting land in return for service – the source of weakness in so many administrations of the time – was replaced with uniform taxation throughout Ottoman domains, avoiding another traditional source of discontent. Islamic law was guaranteed as the law of the land, but only part of the law. In a move that would have significant consequences in the modern era, the Ottomans devised a legal system whereby their legitimacy was maintained. The Ottomans enforced Islamic law, but at the same time they retained the right to issue their own laws for matters not yet developed in Islamic courts. Islamic law, identified as Shariah, was in force side by side with Ottoman law, called Kanun (Arabic: *qanun*). The application of Islamic law was effectively limited to ritual and personal matters (the proper ways to cleanse, pray, give charity, fast, perform pilgrimage, for example, as well as correct procedures for marriage, divorce, inheritance) – which were the most highly developed aspects of Islamic law at the time. That left the Ottoman bureaucracy considerable leeway in developing law for administrative, commercial, and other areas of vital concern to the government. Non-Muslim religious communities – Jews and Christians – were given autonomy, precluding dissent on grounds of religious discrimination.

The stability achieved during this period of Ottoman history allowed for enormous prosperity. Ottoman wealth can perhaps best be measured in its artistic achievements, chief among which are its architectural monuments. Ottoman architecture reached its highpoint during the reign of Suleiman, a generous patron of the arts. His chief architect was Joseph Sinan (d. 1588), a Greek Orthodox citizen drafted into service in his early twenties, who designed hundreds of mosques, palaces, schools, public baths, and poor houses, in addition to bridges, fountains, and granaries. Many of his works are still counted among the most spectacular in the world. Two of the most famous are the great mosques of Suleiman (Suleymaniyya) in Istanbul and Selim in Edirne (Selimiyya). Sinan's buildings are supremely light and elegant. Their enormous central domes and walls are pierced with dozens of windows, and their walls are covered in light colors, inlaid with beautiful tile and mosaic designs. The Mosque of Selim is probably Sinan's greatest achievement. It went beyond his previous technique of achieving lightness and spaciousness through minimal internal supports, to doing away with any internal supports whatsoever. It is not only a monument to architectural beauty; it is an engineering masterpiece.

Plate 3   The Mosque of Selim complex (1557) in Istanbul. © Chris Hellier/ Corbis.

The stability and prosperity of Ottoman administration also allowed for further expansion. From their Egypt base of operations, the Ottomans expanded their authority over the numerous autonomous regimes in North Africa (the Maghreb). By the end of Suleiman's reign their empire included Libya and Algeria (Tunisia would be included soon afterwards). To the Europeans, Suleiman came to be known as "the Magnificent," as he continued Ottoman expansion in their direction. Belgrade fell to Ottoman forces in 1521 and twenty years later, so did Hungary. By 1529, Suleiman's army was besieging Vienna. Although Suleiman's westward expansion was stopped at Vienna, the Ottomans were powerful enough to take advantage of Europe's divided politics. The sixteenth century was a time when Catholics were battling with Protestants, and ruling families were competing for control of the disintegrating Holy Roman Empire. The Habsburgs, still holding the title of Holy Roman emperors, reigned supreme in Austria, the Netherlands, Luxembourg, Burgundy, and Spain. France, naturally, felt surrounded. The French were therefore happy to support Suleiman's efforts in the East, hoping it would weaken the Habsburgs. It was this combination of circumstances that allowed Suleiman's forces to take Belgrade in 1521.

The Habsburgs and Ottomans continued to compete for Hungary for another twenty years, and Europe continued to fear the Ottoman expansion right through the seventeenth century, when the last attempt to take Vienna was turned back. By that time, the Ottoman Empire was well into its declining years, although it would survive until the end of World War I. With the Ottoman Empire, the caliphate survived. The last person to be named caliph, Abdulmecid II, died in exile in Paris in 1924; the office of caliphate was officially abolished in 1924. But despite the caliphal title, and the greatness achieved by the Ottomans, the Muslim world never again achieved political unity. From their stronghold in Anatolia, the Ottoman Turks consolidated control only over the Arab world. The Persian world organized independently.

Persia: The Safavid Empire

While Ottoman expansion was halted in Europe at Vienna, its eastward push was stopped in Persia, which would establish the second great Islamic empire of the middle period. It is arguable that if Suleiman had concentrated all his efforts in the Islamic world instead of pushing into Europe, Islamic political reunification might have been possible. But as it was, Suleiman ended up fighting on two fronts. In the East, he pushed beyond Syria, taking Iraq and parts of Azerbaijan. There he ran up against the expanding power of the Persian shah (king) Esmail and his son Tahmasp I.

After the destruction of Baghdad (1258), various Mongol dynasties established their regimes in the region, and competed for control of the area. Not surprisingly, it was Timur Lang who came out on top, taking Khurasan and eastern Persia by 1385. From there he continued to consolidate his holdings in the region, as we saw above. But while the warrior Seljuks were able to gain dominance in Baghdad and Syria, giving way eventually to the warrior Ottomans, in Persia it was the descendants of a religious order, the Safavids, who were able to oust the Mongols. This would give a very different character to Persian history from that of the Turks and Turkish-dominated Arabs.

The Safavids were a Sufi order that originated in Turkic Azerbaijan in the fourteenth century. Identifiable by their red turbans (which is why they were known as Kizilbash, or "Red Heads"), the Safavids attracted followers from throughout Iran as well as its surrounding territories (Syria, eastern Anatolia, the Caucasus, and beyond). As their influence grew, their ideology also developed. During the fifteenth century, they highlighted their distinction from their primarily Sunni neighbors by identifying themselves as a specifically Shii order. Basing their legitimacy on the main branch of Shii Islam, they became more and more powerful, and gradually overcame other local rulers. By the turn of the sixteenth century, they had evicted the Mongols from northern Iran and declared themselves sovereign.

As Safavid influence spread northwestward into eastern Anatolia, the Ottomans decided they had to stop them. Champions of Sunni orthodoxy, the Ottomans considered the Shii and Sufi Safavids to be heretics. Several serious clashes between the Ottomans and Safavids took place in the early sixteenth century. The Ottomans took the challenge so seriously that when their own Sultan Bayezid (r. 1482–1512) began to be attracted to Sufi mysticism, they deposed him. The ferocious Selim I then took up the struggle against the Shii Safavids. The Safavids were no match for his artillery-equipped troops. Still using archers, the Safavids were defeated in 1514 and sent back into their central Persian strongholds. But the Ottomans, also engaged in Europe, were unable to gain further victories against the Safavids. In a treaty signed at Amsaya (1555), Suleiman agreed to leave Azerbaijan and the Caucasus to Persia, and allow Persian pilgrims access to the holy cities of Mecca and Medina, as well as Shii pilgrimage sites in Iraq.

The western Muslim world thus achieved equilibrium, delineated between the Sunni Ottomans (1517–1924) and the Shii Safavids (1501–1722). Shii Islam, now represented in a state, was free to develop its unique character. As noted in Chapter 1, Sunni and Shii Islam differ very little on essential issues. The main difference between the two branches of Islam lies in their respective theories of government and its relationship to prophecy. In Sunni Islam, the death of Prophet Muhammad marked the end of prophecy and the beginning of human beings' responsibility to find ways to implement the Quran's demand for justice, inspired by the Prophet's example, in ever-changing circumstances. In Shii Islam, the death of the Prophet marked the end of prophecy, but not the end of divinely inspired guidance. According to Shii thought, divinely inspired guidance continues through the family of Prophet Muhammad. Therefore, his descendants were the only legitimate successors to the Prophet's earthly leadership. The Prophet's descendants were not prophets, but their interpretations of scripture were authoritative. By contrast, in Sunni Islam legal scholars were charged with the responsibility of interpreting scripture for application in daily life, and the profession of scholarship was open to anyone willing to undertake the requisite training. As it happened, Shiis did not always agree on the identity of the proper descendant. Shiism split during the seventh century over this issue; there had been other disputes earlier and there were other minor splits later on. But the major branch of Shii thought (the Twelvers, *Ithnaashari* Shiis) agrees that the line of Prophet Muhammad's descendants eligible for community leadership ended by the ninth century. The last imam, Muhammad al-Muntazar, will return before the end of the world as the Mahdi, "guided one." The Mahdi will then lead humanity in creating a just society before the end of time and final judgment. Until that time, the last imam exists in a spiritual form (often called "occultation," *al-ghaibah*, in Arabic), and continues to offer guidance to the community through the legal scholars. Until the Mahdi returns, Shii Muslims are instructed to cooperate with their governments and follow the guidance of the scholars.

In the absence of the imam, Sunni and Shii theories of government, therefore, are not terribly different. Shii Islam, however – particularly Twelver Shiism, did develop an ethos or overall character different from that of the dominant Sunnis. This character stems primarily from the fact that the Shii were persecuted by the early Sunnis. The Prophet's grandsons, championed by the Shii, were harassed by the Sunni Umayyads, and the elder, Husayn, was ultimately martyred. As a result, from its earliest days Shii Islam was a voice of vigilance and protest against injustice, and suffering for the cause of justice. As President Mohammad Khatami of Iran put it recently:

In the Muslim world, especially in Iran, whenever oppressed people have risen against tyranny, their activism has been channeled through religion. People have always witnessed the fiery and bloodied face of religious revolutionaries who have risen to fight oppression and despotism.

Our social conscience is replete with memories of the clash of true believers with hypocrites who have used religion to justify people's misery. Our part of the world has witnessed the historical antagonism between truth- and justice-seeking religion and the oppressive and misguided views of religion that have been the tool of oppressors.

Is it not true that in the history of Islam, religion has opposed religious and secular tyranny?[9]

It was during the Safavid period that Twelver Shii Islam's ethos of suffering in the struggle against injustice was institutionalized. The martyrdom of Imam Husayn in 680 by Umayyad troops took place at Karbala on the 10th of Muharram (the first month of the Islamic calendar). Karbala, in Iraq, became – as it remains today – a major pilgrimage site for Shiis. The month of Muharram became a time of mourning (*ta'ziyyah*), similar to Christian Lent, in memory of the suffering of the martyrs. It is still marked by poetry recitations and reenactments of the martyrdom of Husayn, similar to Christian Passion plays.

Safavid Persia also became a place of high cultural achievement. As in Ottoman Turkey, the peace provided by political equilibrium allowed for prosperity and cultural productivity. By the time Islam came to the Persians, they already had a long history of urban society and efficient bureaucracies. In fact, it was a Persian family who organized the Abbasids' bureaucracy for them. The Safavids therefore readily developed an efficient state administration, which was headquartered in Isfahan. The great Safavid Shah Abbas (r. 1588–1629) made Isfahan his capital and set about beautifying it with parks and fountains, and architectural monuments unrivaled to this day. The city is centrally organized around an enormous plaza surrounded by bazaars (*bazaar* is the Persian word for "market"), parks, palaces, schools, and other public buildings. The city is dominated by mosques, including the magnificent mosques of Shah Abbas and Lotfallah. The Lotfallah Mosque is considered one of the world's most beautiful religious buildings. Its façade is covered with tiles of various shades of blue; its graceful Persian-style dome, with an elegant blue floral design on a white background. People who visit the mosque say its overall effect is so awesome as to inspire spirituality even in unbelievers. Shah Abbas also patronized other arts, including one of Persia's most unique contributions, miniature paintings. Among the oldest surviving examples of this exquisite art form are those from Isfahan. Works by the city's undisputed master, Reza Abbasi, are on display at New York's Metropolitan Museum of Art.

Eventually, Safavid leaders succumbed to attacks from powerful neighbors. The last Safavid king was overthrown by an Afghan tribal leader, Mahmud of Kandahar (1732). Eventually, another Persian dynasty would rise, the Qajars, and they would be replaced by the Pahlavis in the twentieth century. But the influence of Safavid culture remained dominant. Among the first tasks undertaken by Reza Shah Pahlavi (r. 1925–41) was restoration of Isfahan's architectural beauty. Persian culture was also undoubtedly influential in shaping the culture of the third great center of Islamic life in the middle period, Mughal India.

India and the Rise of the Mughals

On the eastern borders of Persia was the autonomous Ghaznavid empire. It had arisen during the decline of Samanid control of western Afghanistan. The Samanids were a Persian family who had gained autonomy under Abbasid rule and taken control of much of Afghanistan as well as the great Silk Road cities of Khurasan, Samarkand, and Bukhara, their capital. They were powerful and their reign was prosperous, known for great art and culture. By the eleventh century, the Samanids' border guards, the Seljuks, had taken over control and begun expanding westward. On the eastern side of the empire, another of their former slave guards (Sebuktegin, d. 997) had broken away and established himself as the ruler of Ghazna (present-day Ghazni, Afghanistan). His son Mahmud (d. 1030) then expanded his control. As the Samanids' power decreased, Mahmud took temporary control of parts of Persia, but his major impact was in the other direction. After a series of brutal raids, he gained control across present-day Pakistan. To that Hindu and Buddhist region, he brought what would become the permanent presence of Islam. His raids, particularly those on Hindu temples, also brought him vast wealth. (Mahmud, like Timur after him, was decidedly intolerant of other religions. He perhaps even set an example for the modern-day Taliban in his destruction of other people's religious icons.) He used this wealth to finance cultural development in his realm, particularly Persian high culture. Although he was of Turkic background and anti-Shii religiously, he established Persian as the language of culture in his realm. He also brought in famous scholars such as the scientist al-Biruni and the poet Firdawsi to his court; the final version of Firdawsi's famous epic *Shah Nameh* (Book of Kings) was dedicated to this ruthless ruler. Written in verse form, the Shah Nameh tells the story of Persian history from ancient times to the Arab conquests. It remains a classic of Persian literature.

Successors to Mahmud's power base moved the capital to Lahore, the great ancient city of the Punjab, having lost eastern ground to Persian powers. There they remained for some time, and much of the region became Muslim. Then, around 1190, the Persian Ghurid rulers who had taken control of Ghazna began raids into Indian territory. They ousted the last of Mahmud's successors at Lahore and within ten years began a military campaign right across northern India. It was the slave-warriors ("mamluks") who worked for the Ghurids who ultimately established what would become Islam's lasting power base in India: the Sultanate of Delhi.

As Mahmud had done in Ghazna, once they had established peace the sultans of Delhi brought Persian-influenced Islamic high culture. Poets and artists were welcomed there, and merchants found ready markets. Sufi missionaries brought their mystical teachings, becoming the major source of Islamic religious learning in India. Indigenous Hindu society in the region was divided along caste lines and well established in their localized realms. Muslim rulers had more expansive territorial designs. Free of caste restrictions and offering religious freedom to their subjects, the Muslims became in effect a ruling class. The sultans of Delhi built on the prosperity offered by trade and local agriculture, and were able to expand their sovereignty during the thirteenth and fourteenth centuries. By 1350 they had gained dominance throughout much of the Indian subcontinent.

The Sultanate of Delhi was effectively ended by another of Timur Lang's infamous attacks. This one was particularly brutal. Timur considered Delhi sultans' policy of religious freedom to be unconscionable. For Timur, unlike most Muslims, religious freedom was not an essential feature of Islam; in fact, he was mortally opposed to it. In 1398 his troops destroyed Delhi and massacred its inhabitants. Fortunately for all concerned, however, Timur was dead by 1405, allowing Islam in India to recover from his near-fatal blow. Autonomous Muslim rulers outside Delhi survived, and eventually Islamic power was reconstituted in Delhi, under the Lodi sultans, from the highlands of Afghanistan, in the late fourteenth century.

What would become the great Mughal (i.e., Mongol) Empire in India was begun by Babur (d. 1530). Babur had inherited Timur's Mongol power in Kabul and, in true Mongol fashion, began to look beyond his borders. In 1526 he defeated the Lido sultans and took control of Delhi. But Babur's Mongol successors would overcome their heritage of intolerance. They would foster a culture of inter-religious respect that would allow them to maintain dominance in India until the British took control in the eighteenth century.

The architect of the Mughals' ecumenical culture was Babur's grandson Akbar "the Great" (r. 1556–1605). As we saw, the stability and prosperity of the Ottoman and Safavid empires were established despite the challenges posed by the ferocious Timur. Akbar was the only ruler of the middle period who was a direct descendant of Timur (as well as of Genghis Khan). But, defying his intolerant heritage, he was among Islam's most enlightened rulers. Inheriting control of virtually all of northern India, including present-day Pakistan, Bangladesh, and Afghanistan, Akbar found himself part of not only a cultural minority but a religious one, as well. Muslims were and would remain a minority in India, along with dozens of other minorities – including Christian, Jewish, and Zoroastrian. But Akbar welcomed religious diversity. He established a uniform tax system that did not discriminate against non-Muslims, and incorporated Hindus into his administration. In order to preclude divisive and destructive religious discrimination, he promoted respect for a non-sectarian monotheism (called *din-i ilahi*, "divine religion"). Allowing full expression of the rich cultural heritage of his many diverse subjects, Akbar thus gave rise to one of the most unique and culturally productive regimes in Islamic history.

Although Islamic rule in India ended in the nineteenth century, and hostility between the Hindus and Muslims remains, Mughal architecture is still among the most enduring and cherished of its legacies. The planned city of Fatehpur Sikri, for example, built by Akbar, is a wonder of sixteenth-century engineering. Its monumental gateway clearly reveals the combined Hindu and Islamic styles. It is ornately carved with multiple arches over a post and lintel structure, and opens directly into the Great Mosque of Fatehpur Sikri. Unfortunately, Akbar and his technicians overlooked one essential aspect of life in their planning: water. The city had to be abandoned for lack of water, but it remains a popular tourist attraction. A massive gate – the

Delhi Gate – was a feature of another of Akbar's achievements, the Agra Fort.

Akbar's son and grandson provided even greater architectural monuments to India. Jahangir (r. 1605–27), who was born on the site of Fatehpur Sikri, added to the beauty of the Mughal landscape, creating the Shalimar Gardens in Kashmir, for example. But his greatest devotion was to art. He was a painter himself, and devoted enormous resources to patronizing the arts. Earlier Mughal painting is known for its riotous colors and movement, but Jahangir's artists, known primarily for their portraiture, developed a more delicate, sedate, almost spiritual style. Jahangir's son Shah Jahan (r. 1628–58) continued to support art (examples can be found in Windsor Castle Library), but not to the extent that his father did. He will always be remembered for his architectural monuments. Among them are the Great Mosque and Red Fort at Delhi – a massive structure of red sandstone, with rows and rows of columns and arches under a flat roof. He also built the Shalimar Gardens of Lahore, eighty acres of lush gardens beautifully landscaped and accented by reflecting pools and fountains of white marble. But none is more famous than the Taj Mahal, the splendid mausoleum he commissioned at Agra for his wife Mumtaz Mahal. Its white marble dome and towers, complemented by its trademark reflecting pool, remain a symbol of love and spirituality for people of all faiths and none.

The respect for religious diversity institutionalized by early Mughal rulers certainly contributed to the peace and prosperity of the realm, reflected in its refined cultural achievements. The period is also noteworthy for its intellectual sophistication. In Mughal India science and scholarship continued to flourish. A unique reflection of this openness and sophistication is in the genre of humorous social satire. An example is found in the stories of Raja Birbal, Emperor Akbar's court poet. Birbal was a peasant from outside Agra who had helped the emperor find his way to Agra one day. In gratitude, the emperor invited the boy to visit him someday in his capital. When he was a bit older,

Birbal decided the time had come. He approached the guards at the royal court and found them skeptical, to say the least. He managed to convince them to let him in, only by promising to share half of any gift the emperor might bestow on the young man. He entered Akbar's chamber and the king remembered him at once and was delighted he had come. "Ask for anything your heart desires and it shall be yours," he said. Birbal said, "If [Your Majesty] pleases, my dearest wish is to be given fifty lashes of the whip!" Naturally, people thought he was crazy but when the king asked him why he wanted such a strange gift, Birbal explained that the guards would only let him in if he split any gift with them. "Are our people to be kept away by a greedy, wicked guard?" thundered the king. "Send for the rascal!" The guard was sentenced to the entire gift of fifty lashes and never again tried to bully poor people who sought an audience with the emperor. And Birbal was given a place at the court, with all the comforts that went with it. "We confer on you the title of Raja Birbal from this day on," the emperor declared. "And you shall stay near us and amuse and guide us hence forth!"[10] From then on, Birbal both entertained and gently criticized the mighty and meek alike.

Even more interesting as a reflection of the times are the stories of Nasroddin. Nasroddin was a legendary figure who symbolized both wisdom and foolishness, or perhaps wisdom and social commentary disguised as foolishness. Satire of any aspect of society could be clothed in a story about Nasroddin. If the story were cleverly enough presented, it might circulate far and wide as a vehicle of people's concerns.

One of the stories told about Nasroddin reveals a growing concern about the excessive mysticism in Indian popular religion. According to the story, Nasroddin was sent by the king to find out about the spiritual leaders who had become famous in India at the time. Nasroddin traveled the countryside, interviewing members of the mystical communities, and listening as they outdid one another with stories of their leaders' wondrous and miraculous works. He then returned home and wrote his report for the king. It contained only one word: "Carrots." The king asked him what that was supposed to mean. What do carrots have to do with mysticism? Nasroddin explained that like a carrot, most of the reality of mysticism is hidden from view; very few people recognize it when they see it growing; it must be cultivated and if not, it will deteriorate; and "there are a great many donkeys associated with it."[11]

In fact, Islam in India had traditionally been dominated by Sufi teachers, particularly those from the Chishti and Suhrawardi orders. Islamic political sovereignty in the Indian subcontinent was established by military forces. But spreading the religion itself was left primarily to the Sufi preachers. The Chishtis began in India in the twelfth century. Deeply spiritual, Chishti preachers taught people to avoid materialism in all its forms. Poverty was considered a virtue and social involvement a distraction. The goal of spiritual life in Chishti thought was to achieve union with the divine One by transcending the self through chanting (*dhikr*, a common Sufi practice consisting of rhythmic repetition of the names of God or short prayers) and meditation. Chishti communal centers (khanaqahs) became major sources of Islamic teaching from the thirteenth and fourteenth centuries in northern India – for many people, they were the only source of Islamic teaching. The Suhrawardi order was likewise extremely spiritual. Its teachings are based on those of Shihab al-Din al-Suhrawardi (d. 1191), who was put to death (he is therefore often called al-Maqtul, "the Killed") for teachings that were judged to blur the distinction between God and creatures. Suhrawardi described existence as light; all individual existents ("creatures" in ordinary language) are like rays, ever dimmer, emanating from the One, Pure Light, God. The goal of spiritual development is to move ever closer to the Source, eventually losing all individuality by being reunited with it. (For this reason, al-Suhrawardi is called a philosopher of Illumination, *hikmat al-ishraq*.) The mystical approaches of these orders seemed to some to have deviated almost completely from basic Islamic teachings. Some Sufis even disregarded the Shariah (Islamic law, including the Five Pillars), in favor of guidance from their Sufi masters (teachers).

This approach to spiritual development allowed for a wide range of religious expression and was, as such, naturally tolerant. But it also gave rise to concern among scholars that the essential roots of Islamic teaching were being lost. They were afraid that Islam's core teachings were being replaced with an amalgam of religious and spiritual teachings, and that many of them were distinctly un-Islamic. For example, al-Suhrawardi taught that religious differences are unimportant. They are simply some of the many manifestations of divinity; as people develop spiritually, they transcend these differences. This approach to religious diversity obviously undermined the importance of Islam as a distinct religion – a development that was bound to displease religious authorities. Beyond that, however, the belief that all reality is in fact one seemed to be heretical. It was contrary to Islamic monotheism. Traditional religious scholars believed that it contradicted the Islamic view that God is the Creator of all individuals, and that there is eternally an essential distinction between God and creatures. To claim that human beings share in any way in divinity seemed to be not only heretical but blasphemous. In fact, this monism (belief that all existence is essentially unified) appeared to some scholars to be influenced by Hinduism. After all, Hindus, despite their multiplicity of gods, believe that in reality, there is only One, one reality in which all individual existents – inanimate, animate, divine – participate. Traditional religious scholars therefore began to feel the need to root out what they considered un-Islamic influences.

The concern for orthodoxy in Indian Islam showed itself as early as the sixteenth century, in response to the growing popularity of a new religion that seemed to combine Islam and Hinduism: Sikhism. There had been significant interaction between Hindu and Islamic spirituality. Many spiritual exercises of Hindu yoga practice – controlled breathing patterns, for example, and the use of meditation to achieve heightened religious awareness – found their way into Sufi practice, and Islamic monotheism found increasing expression in otherwise polytheistic Hindu thought. But Sikhism was a new religious movement that actively blended characteristically Islamic monotheism with Hindu monism. The Sikh religion was begun by Guru Nanak (d. 1539), a Hindu spiritual teacher from the Punjab (in northwest India). It combined elements of both Hindu and Islamic teaching. For instance, Nanak taught that there is only one God, but also that people undergo countless rebirths on the road to *moksha* (escape from the cycle of rebirth) and reabsorption into the divine One. Nanak taught that people can escape that cycle through virtuous living and meditation on God's name. Both Muslim and Hindu scholars found fault with Nanak's teachings, but their popularity continued to spread under Nanak's successors, especially in the tolerant atmosphere created by Akbar. But during the reign of Jahangir, concern for religious orthodoxy began to gain political attention. At this time, leadership of the Sikh community had passed to Nanak's fifth successor, Arjun. In response to scholars' complaints, Jahangir demanded that Arjun remove references from Sikh scriptures that were offensive to either Muslims or Hindus. When Arjun refused, he was tortured to death (1606).

There were even Sufis who believed that some mystics went too far. Sheikh Ahmad Sirhindi (d. 1625) was one of them. He was a leader in another Sufi order, the Naqshbandis, a more reserved order from Central Asia. Sirhindi was appalled by Emperor Akbar's religious initiatives, particularly his eclectic new "divine religion" (*din-i ilahi*). He believed Akbar's and Jahangir's religious openness was dangerous to Islam, and did not even think Shii Muslims should be tolerated. But his most vehement criticisms were directed toward Chishtis and anyone else who believed that all existence is really One. He taught that this belief in the unity of existence (*wahdat al-wujud*) was really just a deceptive misperception resulting from an altered state of consciousness achieved through "artificial means" (the various exercises such as chanting and rhythmic swaying). Sirhindi criticizes the Sufis, saying that it only seems that all unity is One (*wahdat al-shuhud*, oneness of appearances); despite the appearance of unity in mystical consciousness, in reality creatures remain distinct from one another, as well as from the Creator. To claim that this perception is actually the way things are is heresy, since it equates God with his creatures. What is more, people who claim that all existence is One, and that everything that exists is really a manifestation of God, also do away with evil, since God is necessarily all good. For this kind of Sufi, then, evil is just a perception, too. In this context, Sirhindi says, the law of God becomes irrelevant. Straying from the Shariah, he concludes, people naturally fall into moral decline.

Jahangir thought Sirhindi's intolerance of Sufis was misguided. He had him imprisoned for a short time. But Sirhindi had obviously struck a sympathetic chord among many Muslims, and he became widely popular. He was declared *Mujaddid al-Alf al-Thani*, "the renewer of the second millennium" of Islam. Sirhindi also influenced some Mughals, in particular Akbar's great grandson Aurangzeb (r. 1659–1707). When Aurangzeb was young, Sufism was still highly influential among the Mughals. His own brother, Dara Shikoh (d. 1659) – next in line for their father Shah Jahan's throne, was among them. Drawn to mysticism, Dara Shikoh promoted the esoteric teachings of many religions. He surrounded himself with people of many faiths, and personally sponsored translation of Hindu scriptures. Aurangzeb took it upon himself to champion the cause of orthodoxy, first within his own family. He and two other brothers – all provincial governors – fought with Dara Shikoh for the right to take control of the empire. Dara's troops defeated one brother's army. Then the two remaining brothers joined forces, defeating Aurangzeb's imperial forces in a series of battles. Aurangzeb then had Dara Shikoh executed as a heretic; the two other brothers were exiled and killed. Finally, Aurangzeb had himself declared emperor. His sickly father was imprisoned, where he died seven years later.

This violent beginning of Aurangzeb's reign was only a taste of what was to come. Like his predecessors, Aurangzeb insisted on expanding Mughal control militarily, leading to numerous and ongoing rebellions that drained the Mughal resources during Aurangzeb's long reign. Internally, Aurangzeb began a campaign to impose Islam, in its traditional form, throughout the realm. That meant reversing many of Akbar's policies that had led to peaceful relations with non-Muslim religious communities, especially Hindus. He re-imposed the tax on non-Muslims, had many Hindu temples and schools destroyed and prohibited the building of new ones or even repairing old ones. He imposed economic policies that disadvantaged Hindus, and offered bribes to those who would convert to Islam. Naturally, these policies marginalized and alienated Hindus, fatally weakening the social fabric of Mughal India.

Aurangzeb's relations with the Sikhs were no better than with the Hindus. After Arjun's execution under Jahangir, the Sikhs had retreated from their pacifist stance and established themselves in a defensive position in the Punjab. In its largest city, Lahore, Aurangzeb built the colossal Badshahi Mosque. It is one of the world's largest, to symbolize the triumph of Islam. Aurangzeb also tried to force the Sikh guru Tegh Bahadur to convert to Islam. When he refused, Aurangzeb had him executed. This resulted in further militarization of the Sikh community, and further hostility toward the Muslim rulers. This hostility often flared into open rebellions against their Muslim overlords in the Punjab, resulting in a cycle of vicious reprisals.

Succeeding Mughal leaders thus inherited a mortally wounded realm. Continued efforts to impose Islamic dominance on a mixed population, with a Hindu majority, resulted in ongoing uprisings and inter-communal warfare in India. Indeed, it was these rebellions that allowed Britain to impose direct rule over much of the subcontinent in 1857. They held it until 1947, when it

Plate 4 Worshippers at Badshahi Mosque in Lahore. © World Religions Picture Library/Christine Osborne.

was partitioned by the United Nations into the Hindu-majority state of India, and the Muslim-majority state of Pakistan.

Understanding Developments in Islamic History

Following the classical period of Islam, when its texts and ideals were formulated and its basic institutions established, Muslims were subjected to a number of attacks – by plague and disease, but more importantly, by foreign invaders. The once unified Muslim community became fragmented. After the decline of the Abbasid caliphate, Muslims would never again live as a single political unit. A period of division and almost continuous warfare was followed by reorganization. The Muslim world reconstituted itself into the three empires discussed above – the Ottoman, the

Safavid, and the Mughal – as well as several other autonomous Islamic communities in sub-Saharan Africa and South Asia. Still, Muslim intellectuals felt the need to put these developments into perspective. Thirteenth-century historian Ibn al-Athir registered the concern of many that infighting among regional rulers was weakening the Islamic community. He believed that it was the infighting that allowed the foreigners to be successful: "It was the discord between the Muslim princes . . . that enabled the Franks [Crusaders] to overrun the country."[12] There is no question that Ibn al-Athir was right. We saw that the majority of the battles fought by the Ottomans, Safavids, and Mughals were against Muslims, as they jockeyed for position in the vacuum created by the decline of Abbasid power.

Yet we also saw that – when stability was restored – Islamic society continued to be prosperous and enormously creative. Many of the great scientific and artistic achievements described above were achieved not under the unified Umayyad or Abbasid caliphates, but under the various regional units that developed after the demise of central authority. Many of the great thinkers and artists of the time ended up working under a number of different patrons, depending upon the political situation. There is the famous case of Nasr al-Din al-Tusi (d. 1274). Al-Tusi was the renowned Persian astrologer and mathematician who developed the most accurate table of planetary motion known to science at the time. He did it while working at the great observatory at Maragheh in Azerbaijan, which he himself commissioned to be built while he was a government minister under the Mongol leader Hulegu Khan. That was after he had worked under a branch of the Shiis known as the Ismailis. When they were attacked by the Mongols – some say with al-Tusi's assistance – al-Tusi, who was actually a Twelver Shii, joined the Mongols and encouraged them to destroy Sunni Baghdad in 1258.

The great historian Ibn Khaldun (d. 1406) also had experience working under a number of regimes, from Spain to North Africa and Egypt. But he used his experience as a laboratory for understanding political and historical processes in general. As we saw in Chapter 2, Ibn Khaldun's *Muqaddimah* (Introduction [to the History of the Arabs, Persians, and Berbers]) is often cited as the first work of historiography and precursor to the modern studies of anthropology, sociology, economics, and political science. But he is perhaps best known for his theory of the cycles or patterns of power. In Ibn Khaldun's view, the rise and fall of regimes is perfectly natural. His analysis is based on the world in which he lived, which was divided between nomads of the deserts and settled peoples of the towns. In his view, nomadic communities have a natural solidarity (*asabiyyah*) resulting from the difficult lifestyle. They have to cooperate and assist one another or they will not survive. When a group of nomads decides to give up their wandering ways and settle in towns, their natural solidarity and expectation of cooperation in the face of challenges serves them well. It translates into a commitment to fairness and mutual assistance, both necessary for the continued survival of the group. But that solidarity only lasts for one or two generations in a settled environment. The settled life is easier than the nomadic life, and people get lazy. The first few generations remember how difficult life was in the desert and work hard to maintain balance and order within their new domestic environment. But as prosperity develops, the natural solidarity fades. People forget how important fairness and cooperation are, and begin to work for personal gain. This results in competition and rivalries that divide the community against itself and inevitably leave it weakened and open for conquest.

The world in which Ibn Khaldun lived was a perfect example of this cycle. He was surrounded by competing regimes – and survived a number of them. But unlike political analysts, Ibn Khaldun did not equate the strength of the Muslim community with political or military power. Instead, he identified the source of strength of the Muslim community as its commitment to justice. As long as the members of the community remained committed to justice – which consisted in an ethic of fairness and cooperation among community members, the community would remain strong. When community members turn against each other, putting their own interests above those of the group, the social fabric is weakened and eventually splits. "Injustice," he said, "brings about the ruin of civilization":

> Whoever takes someone's property, or uses him for forced labor, or presses an unjustified claim against him, or imposes upon him a duty not required by the religious law, does an injustice to that particular person. People who collect unjustified taxes commit an injustice. Those who infringe upon property commit an injustice. Those who take away property commit an injustice. Those who deny people their rights commit an injustice. Those who, in general, take property by force, commit an injustice. It is the dynasty that suffers from all these acts, inasmuch as civilization, which is the substance of the dynasty, is ruined when people have lost all incentive. This is what Muhammad actually had in mind when he forbade injustice.

Ibn Khaldun then concludes with a justification for the preservation of human rights as articulated in classical Islam: "This is what the religious law quite generally and wisely aims at in emphasizing five things as necessary: the preservation of (1) religion, (2) the soul (life), (3) the intellect, (4) progeny, and (5) property."[13]

For Ibn Khaldun, the ultimate purpose of the Islamic community was justice. God established the Muslim community and commissioned them – as his stewards – to spread justice throughout the world, by protecting people's rights to religion, life, education, family, and property. Commitment to this purpose was to be the basis of their solidarity (*asabiyyah*). When that commitment weakened among various rulers, inevitably their regimes fell into decline.

But Islamic civilization as a whole need not decline, provided people maintain their commitment to justice. Ibn Khaldun actually chastises people in his era who take a passive attitude toward establishing justice. These are the people who sit back and wait for the Mahdi to appear. Ibn Khaldun says that all Muslims believe that at the end of time a man from the family of Prophet Muhammad will appear and lead Muslims back to a just society. Because the society will be just, it will also be powerful. The Mahdi and/or Jesus will then overpower the Antichrist, ushering in years of justice before the Final Judgment. (The Mahdi is not mentioned in the Quran. Belief in the Mahdi comes from oral traditions, which are not consistent. That is why some people believe that Jesus will come after the Antichrist appears so that he can do away with him, while others believe that Jesus will come with the Mahdi and help him get rid of the Antichrist.) Ibn Khaldun notes that some scholars criticize belief in the Mahdi, although he himself does not. But he does criticize people in his own time who simply assume that injustice will be corrected soon, when the Mahdi appears.[14] He believes all people must work for justice by maintaining their commitment to fairness and cooperation in all their social dealings. In the same way, he criticizes people who rely on fortune tellers and astrologers to predict the future. (He uses as evidence of their unreliability the fact that at the time of Prophet Muhammad, there were reports that the world would end 500 years after the coming of Prophet Muhammad. Ibn Khaldun was born 723 years after the Hijra.)

Instead of waiting for the Mahdi or allowing fortune tellers to control their destiny, Ibn Khaldun says people should use reason to understand their religion and the world, and figure out how to establish Islamic values in the world's ever-changing circumstances. Furthermore, he criticizes those mystics who believe that all of existence is One, that only God exists and we are all a part of God. He says that is just a passing perception, and it is foolish to trust such passing perceptions, like blind people who are not aware that there is an entire dimension of perception beyond their limited abilities.

Rather than trying to understand things beyond their perceptive abilities, people should concentrate on things they can understand. Ibn Khaldun then gives an elegant description of empirical science, the kind of understanding of their environment that human beings can develop through observation and reasoning in an orderly way. Pursuit of science has obvious practical uses that promote human well-being. Practical sciences can help us build better homes, for example, and grow better crops. But of all the kinds of science, law is the most important, since it details the ways to promote justice and prevent injustice. And this is the purpose for which human beings were created.

Conclusion

Ibn Khaldun's analysis of the rise and fall of nations was brilliant. It became a classic of historiography. And his articulation of the source of strength of Islam is an eloquent tribute to Islamic values. But it still leaves unanswered the question of Islamic trauma in the modern era. How did the Muslim world – the world of Suleiman the Magnificent, Shah Abbas, and Akbar the Great, the world of universities and public libraries, great architects and artists, literature and learning – become part of what is today known as the Third World – weak, underdeveloped, and associated with unpopular governments? How did these magnificent states of the middle period of Islamic history become subjected to European powers? That is the question addressed in the following chapters.

Chapter 4

Colonialism and Reform

The twentieth century was disastrous for the Muslim world. It opened with European powers in control of large portions of former Ottoman and Mughal lands, as well as other parts of the Muslim world, and dominating in Iran. World War I ended the caliphate and consolidated European control over most of the Muslim world. Muslims in all these regions therefore had to struggle with multiple challenges and against enormous odds. As the vitality of Muslim society declined, reformers had begun to work in many parts of the Muslim world. But their work was complicated by the threat of foreign domination. A number of trends thus emerged: agitation for reform in declining Islamic empires, the struggle for independence from growing European power, efforts to modernize Islamic societies and reform religious thought in order to deal with contemporary challenges. In this chapter we will survey the takeover of the Muslim world by European powers, and examine the early reform movements meant to deal with it.

Colonialism

By the early twentieth century, almost the entire Muslim world was under the control of European countries. The French controlled all across North Africa and Syria; the British controlled Egypt, Palestine, Iraq, and India; the Dutch controlled Indonesia; and the Dutch and then the British controlled Malaysia. From that vantage point, it began to look like the Crusades were on again. But it took some time before the pattern of colonization became clear, because the process of Europe's gaining control of these regions was actually gradual and, in some cases, subtle. It also developed sporadically, one city or region at a time, over a wide range of geographic areas. Spain established a beachhead here; France set up control there; Britain took over areas in North Africa, the Middle East, and in India; Italy and Holland operated at opposite ends of the Islamic world; and so on. European countries gained control of the Muslim world through a combination of strategies, including gradual assumption of economic power, playing off internal rivals against one another, and military campaigns when necessary. As a result, Europe's overall domination of the Muslim world did not become apparent to most people until it was almost complete.

After the Crusades, the first European inroads were by way of the sea, when the Portuguese took control of the Indian Ocean spice trade from the Arabs. As we saw in Chapter 3, this was a wound to the Mamluk economy from which it never recovered. Eventually, the Ottomans were able to overpower the Mamluks and take control of almost the entire Arab world. For centuries, the Ottomans had been a formidable power. They were powerful enough to be able to play a role in Europe's pre-modern power struggles, when regional powers struggled to assert themselves against the old imperial families who wanted to control the entire continent. We saw above how Suleiman the Magnificent was able to manipulate those struggles to Ottoman advantage in the Balkans. However, in the bargain Suleiman gave French subjects the right to travel and trade in Ottoman lands. French traders were also given the protection of French laws and courts even while they were in Ottoman lands; they were exempted from Ottoman laws, including taxes. Suleiman also granted the French King Francis I the right to control access to trade in the Middle East for other European subjects (Capitulations of 1536).

These special privileges (*imtiyazat*) were later demanded by the British, as well, and expanded throughout the Ottoman Empire. They assured the Europeans safety of life and property, and freedom of religion, but the exemption from Ottoman law and taxes also gave the Europeans distinct trade advantages. These trade advantages, later obtained by the Europeans in the Persian world, as well, were often passed on to local Christian and Jewish communities. They proved to be the critical factors in the Capitulations. They allowed Europeans and their allies in the Muslim world greater wealth than was possible for local Muslims to obtain.

Obviously, the brilliant Suleiman would not have given the Europeans such rights if they had posed any threat at the time. But, as it turned out, French cultural and economic influence in Syria (which included Lebanon until after World War I) grew exponentially. Religious missions were founded by Roman Catholics, catering to the area's Christians and others interested in the advantages provided by European learning. European merchants had established lucrative trade in Syrian cotton, silks, and handicrafts by the seventeenth and eighteenth centuries. But soon the balance of trade began to shift. European manufactured goods were being imported, replacing indigenous crafts and enriching those merchants with close relations to Europe. By the late nineteenth century, it began to appear to Syria's Muslim majority that the Christians (including the Orthodox, who had benefited from Russian missions) were developing a distinct advantage based on foreign support. Communal conflicts erupted into riots, bringing increased attention from both Ottoman officials and Europeans. Foreign influence continued to expand. France built rail connections between Syria's three major cities – Damascus, Beirut, and Aleppo. The American University of Beirut (originally called the Syrian Protestant College) was established in 1866, and the French Jesuit Université Saint-Joseph opened in Beirut in 1881.

By the outbreak of World War I, Christians were among Syria's most highly educated and Western-influenced population, and France treated the region as part of its eminent domain. In the Versailles Treaty ending that war, France was granted "mandate" control over Syria that would not end until France was occupied by Nazi Germany in World War II and could no longer afford to manage its Syrian territories.

By that time, France – locked into competition with other European colonial powers – had already taken control of Morocco, Algeria, and Tunisia. In 1830, France attacked Algiers, technically part of the Ottoman Empire but virtually autonomous. The French proclaimed that they had nothing against the people of Algeria, only their Turkish rulers. Their original complaint was against piracy, a venerable tradition in the Mediterranean. Mediterranean piracy had been practiced by the Greeks, Romans, and Carthaginians. The famous Barbary pirates (named after the non-Arab inhabitants of North Africa, the Berbers) followed the same practice, demanding tribute from ships seeking to pass through their waters and seizing them along with their crews and all their contents if they refused. This provided a ready source of funds in their efforts to maintain their independence from Istanbul. But it was not popular among the nations whose economies were increasingly dependent upon sea trade. The practice became so unpopular that European countries and the newly formed United States demanded a halt to it and fought several battles when the pirate states refused. President Thomas Jefferson even sent the navy which struggled with the pirates for four years (Tripolitan War, 1801–05). The British had bombed Algeria in 1816 in an effort to stop piracy, and had largely been successful. Nevertheless, the French claimed that their goal in attacking Algiers in 1830 was to put a stop to piracy. Their attack was successful, and the Ottoman officials were sent packing. But the French did not leave. The region quickly attracted French settlers and France appointed a "governor general of the French possessions in Africa," headquartered in Algiers. Resistance by Algerians began immediately, but it only intensified the French resolve to take full control of the area. After years of Algerian attacks on settlers' farms and French reprisals against Algerian villages, France declared itself the ruler of Algeria. In 1845 Paris appointed a "governor general of Algeria." By 1871 Algerian resistance was crushed. Algeria was considered a part of France. It only regained independence after a brutal war for independence (1954–62), in which an estimated one-tenth of the population lost their lives and another one-fifth to one-third were displaced (relocated by the French).

From its North African headquarters in Algeria, France was able to expand its control to include Morocco. Morocco had never been a part of the Ottoman Empire, enjoying independence that allowed it to be a refuge for Algerians fleeing the wrath of France. But Moroccan assistance to the struggling Algerian resistance brought French attacks. The French military easily defeated the Moroccans in the 1840s. But the European powers were always in competition for colonial holdings, the source of enormous wealth for these industrializing powers. So in the 1850s, Britain negotiated for special trading privileges in Morocco, promising to protect Moroccans from the French. Meanwhile, Spain claimed territories in the western portion of Morocco, and declared war to secure them. Morocco had suffered under a succession of weak rulers in the late nineteenth century. This led to rebellions that further weakened the sultan and allowed the Europeans to press their own claims. In a classic example of European colonial gamesmanship, Britain, Spain, and Italy agreed in 1904 to let France take over in Morocco if France let England have Egypt, Spain exercise its influence over northwestern Morocco, and Italy take Libya. A futile rebellion by the sultan's brother ended in the Treaty of Fez (1912) which declared Morocco a French protectorate.

Meanwhile, on the other side of Algeria, Tunisia also asserted autonomy from its nominal Ottoman overlords. But Tunisia also felt threatened by its much larger neighbor Algeria. So when the French came into Algeria in 1830, Tunisia accepted their offer to act on their behalf in the rule of Algeria. When it became clear that France actually intended to take direct control in Algeria, Tunisian rulers recognized the threat to their own independence and desperately tried to strengthen themselves against the modern European power. But they could only attempt this by raising taxes and taking out loans – from Europe. Popular discontent erupted in rebellions that further strained government resources. The Europeans finally decided to take control of Tunisia's government in order to recoup their debts. The only real suspense was over which of Tunisia's major lenders – Britain or France – would take ultimate control. The European colonial powers each worried that the other was taking unfair advantage in placing their increasingly high-stakes claims in the disintegrating Ottoman Empire. They came together at the Congress of Vienna in 1878 to deal with a number of related issues. One of the outcomes was that Britain gave France permission to take control in Tunisia. On the pretext of securing Algeria's borders, France set up a resident governor in Tunisia and assumed direct control in 1881. France kept control of Morocco and Tunisia until 1956, officially, but in reality kept control of certain strategic areas until the 1960s.

Meanwhile, Britain had been extremely busy establishing its global empire. India became the jewel in England's imperial crown by processes similar to France's occupation of Syria. By the end of the fifteenth century, as we saw, Portugal had achieved dominance in trade in the Indian Ocean, by virtue of the superiority of their sea routes over the Arab land routes. By the seventeenth century, the British, French, and Dutch were competing for trade advantage in the region. The British East India Company, established by royal charter in 1600 specifically to gain control of trade in India and points east, acted as more than a commercial enterprise. Like what we now call "multi-national" or "transnational" corporations, it is difficult to say whether the British East India Company acted as an agent of British power or vice versa. Either way, the effect on India was the same. In order to achieve its monopolistic goals, the Company required military force, as well as administrators to control foreign populations, and the government was happy to oblige. In 1612 British forces defeated Portugal in battle and won concessions from the Mughals to engage in trade in cotton, silk, indigo, and spices. A rival British company struggled with the East India Company and in the early eighteenth century, the two merged into the United Company of Merchants of England. This was during the time when Mughal power was declining; the intolerant policies of the successors of Akbar were increasingly unpopular and regional powers struggled to assert their autonomy. The resulting weaknesses in various regions of India provided opportunities for the United Company. It gained control of Bengal in 1757 and from there began to expand, defeating the forces of the Mughals, regional forces, and other colonial competitors and, overall, exploiting the weaknesses in the subcontinent caused by disputes among the Mughals and their Hindu enemies.

The British government soon acted to take control from the Company of what was effectively its policy in India, and continued the policy of expanding British control. Decisive defeats of local forces in 1818 brought capitulations from other leaders. India was no longer the home of the Mughal Empire; it had gradually shifted from being a British trade monopoly to being a British colony. In 1846 the British defeated the Sikhs, who had established a state in the Punjab (northwest India) in the late eighteenth century. They annexed Sikh territory in 1849. The final stage came in 1857. By that time, Britain controlled, either directly or through compliant local leaders, virtually all of India. A revolt erupted among Bengali troops employed by the British.

The immediate cause of the rebellion reflects the widespread discontent among all Indians – Muslim and Hindu – caused by British disruption of traditional life and imposition of foreign values. The British had ordered the troops to use a new kind of rifle. But in order to load the rifle, the end of the cartridges had to be bitten off. The trouble was that the soldiers believed that the grease on the cartridges was a mixture of both cow and pig fat, so both Hindus and Muslims were offended. The British were so unpopular overall, however, that the revolt quickly spread to Delhi and turned into a general rebellion against British rule. It took over a year, but the British were able to put down the rebellion and institute direct rule of the subcontinent. By then, it was said that "the sun never sets on the British empire." (Their colonial subjects explained that that was because God couldn't trust the British in the dark.) They did not leave until 1947, when they "partitioned" the subcontinent into the majority Hindu state of India and the Islamic state of Pakistan, consisting of two sections (East Pakistan and West Pakistan) separated by languages and culture and over one thousand miles of India. The status of Kashmir, a Muslim majority state ruled by a Hindu, has never been settled.

At the same time, Britain was gaining control of Egypt and Sudan. Napoleon had sailed into the port of Alexandria, Egypt in 1798, and announced to the Egyptian people that he was going to overthrow the Mamluks, who had regained autonomy in Egypt. He claimed that the Mamluks were unworthy to rule Egypt because they were not good Muslims. He then told them that the French were better Muslims than the Mamluks, and his proof was that the French had destroyed the power of the pope, who had called the Crusades, and then evicted the notoriously anti-Muslim crusader knights from Malta. The French then occupied Egypt, saying that they were protecting the Egyptians from the Turks, too, whose greed had destroyed Egypt. Although Napoleon may have believed himself, it seemed to the Egyptians that his real goals were more mundane. They included protection of French trade, already well established there as it had been in Syria due to the favorable trade conditions provided to Europeans by the Capitulations. As well, the reliability of Egypt's annual grain production was attractive, given the periodic shortages at home. The French administrators of Egypt set about modernizing Egypt in their own image. Their new bureaucracy established new tax policies and began confiscating Mamluk lands and redistributing them to those who would support their administration. They also built hospitals and made other contributions to the country, but they were still intruders and their continued occupation met with stiff local resistance.

By 1801 the French had to vacate Egypt, after the Ottoman military defeated them in a series of battles, assisted by a British naval blockade. (They took with them the Rosetta Stone, which their archaeologists had discovered, providing the key to deciphering the pyramids' hieroglyphics. They took other ancient Egyptian artifacts as well, which would become the inspiration for a new style in French design motifs: art deco.) One of the leaders of the Ottoman campaign, Mehmed (Muhammad) Ali (d. 1848), was then put in control of Egypt. He tried to reorganize the country in ways that would allow Egypt to regain its pride of place among the world's nations, and secure it against foreign invaders. He totally centralized control of the economy and government, executing the Mamluk chiefs who competed for power and confiscating their properties as well as those endowed through religious foundations (*waqf* properties). He revived and modernized the country's irrigation system, and introduced improved crops for export. He modernized the educational system, using French instructors and advisors and encouraging Egyptians to study abroad. And he modernized the military, initiating a draft so that Egyptians could defend themselves rather than rely on Ottoman troops.

Mehmed Ali also gained independence from Istanbul by using his military to help out in their campaigns against the rebellious

Wahhabis. The Wahhabis were a narrowly traditionalist reform movement in Arabia, bent on reviving the strength of early Islam by wiping out "innovations" like Sufism and art. They were also militant. In their view, contrary to that of other Muslims since the first century of Islam, Muslims who violate their strict rules – for example, by visiting the tombs of holy people and praying for their intercession – were declared infidels who must be fought. The movement is based on the teachings of Muhammad ibn Abd al-Wahhab (d. 1791), and spread by the Saudi family with whom they allied in the mid-eighteenth century. The combined Wahhabi–Saudi forces gained dominance in the Arabian peninsula. When they began to spread northward into Iraq and Syria, the Ottoman sultan asked for and received Mehmed Ali's assistance in confining the movement to the peninsula. Autonomy in Egypt and Sudan, the eastern portion of which he had already conquered, was Mehmed Ali's reward.

Mehmed Ali's successors, though more conservative, continued efforts to develop Egyptian economic power. They wanted to keep their independence from Istanbul, and knew they needed outside help to continue developing. But they were suspicious of Europe's growing influence in the region, so they switched back and forth from the French to the British for assistance. The British built a railway from Alexandria to Suez (1858), which allowed them a faster route to India, for example; the French then built the Suez Canal (1869), making the trip even easier. But all this development was expensive, and much of the capital was borrowed – again, from European sources. Many of the reforms did improve Egypt's financial status. For example, its long staple cotton became extremely valuable when the US civil war eliminated American cotton from the world market. But when the war was over, Egypt was again faced with mounting debt – which would ultimately end the country's independence. By 1875, the Egyptian ruler was forced to sell his shares in the Suez Canal to Britain. The following year an international commission was set up to deal with Egypt's debt – one of the world's first international debt crises. The commission put all Egyptian finances under the control of a British and a French agent. When the Egyptians protested, France and Britain induced the Ottoman sultan to oust the Egyptian ruler (1879). The Europeans took over again, infuriating Egyptians. Opposition groups organized within the National Assembly, which had been established in 1866, and the military, resulting in the establishment of Egypt's first political party, the National Party (*al-Hizb al-Watani*). The French and British sent naval forces to Alexandria in 1882 to protect their investments. Riots erupted and British ships responded by bombing Alexandria and occupying Cairo. Britain kept control of Egypt, declaring it a British "protectorate" at the beginning of World War I, and installing a compliant monarch at the end. Officially, Egypt was independent, but the monarchy implemented British policy. Actual independence was not achieved until a military coup overthrew the monarch in 1952.

Further east, the Dutch secured their hold over Indonesia and, for a time, Malaysia. Islam had been introduced to the Malay peninsula and the islands that would become Malaysia and Indonesia by Indian traders in the thirteenth and fourteenth centuries. By the early sixteenth century, Portuguese merchants were well established in the region's Moluccan Islands, the "Spice Islands." But within a century, the Dutch East India Company outmaneuvered both the Portuguese and local traders and gained control of the region. Apart from a brief interlude of French control (1811–16, when France had conquered Holland and incorporated Indonesia into their empire) and Japanese control (1942–45, during World War II), the Dutch remained in power in Indonesia until 1949. The Dutch were ousted from what would become Malaysia (as well as Singapore) by Britain in the late eighteenth and nineteenth centuries. Except for the Japanese occupation during World War II, they kept control of Malaysia until 1957.

Italy also got into the colonizing act. Like other North African provinces of the Ottoman Empire, Libya had gained semi-autonomy during the eighteenth century. But the Ottomans reasserted direct control in 1835. Meanwhile, Italy began its efforts to compete with other European colonial powers. Britain's theory of colonial expansion tended to focus on coastal areas. Capitalizing on its naval superiority, Britain established bases around the "rims" of continents. France favored a North–South approach, establishing its colonial outposts directly south of its own territory. Italy favored the latter approach and chose Libya as a target for its colonial aspirations. After establishing a number of financial interests in the country, Italy secured direct control of Libya by defeating Ottoman forces in 1912. They consolidated their power in 1932, after destroying Libyan resistance. But then Italy lost control of Libya to British and French administrators until independence was granted by the United Nations in 1951.

The Outcome of World War I

This pattern of European commercial and political expansion spread across the Muslim world. Europe or "the West," as it is now called, did not operate as a unit, following a pre-planned scheme to take control of the whole Muslim world. Individual European countries used the rest of the world – including the Muslim world – as a kind of monopoly board to play out their colonial competition. As one European power moved into one region, another moved into a neighboring region in an effort to block its opponent's expansion. European countries bargained with one another and traded countries in an effort to gain strategic advantage – with utter disregard for the rights and welfare of the countries being traded. The best examples are to be found in the Middle East, particularly Iraq. The land between the two great rivers, the Euphrates and the Tigris, has a long and illustrious history as Mesopotamia, part of the famous Fertile Crescent. But the modern state of Iraq was created by the Europeans from parts of three Ottoman provinces: most of Basra province in the South with its primarily Shii Arab population, Baghdad in the center with its predominantly Sunni Arab population, and parts of Mosul in the North, with its Sunni Kurdish population. (Kurds are a linguistic/ethnic group distinct from Arabs, Persians, and Turks.) The region had come under Ottoman rule in the sixteenth century but, as we have seen, Ottoman power was in steep decline by the beginning of the twentieth century. The Persian Gulf had been familiar territory to European traders since the early seventeenth century. But the discovery of oil in Iraq sharpened competition for this corner of Ottoman territory.

By the early twentieth century, the Ottoman sultan had been dubbed "the sick man of Europe." He was pictured in cartoons as a carcass, over which European-named vultures circled. Among those predators were Britain, Holland, and Germany – or more precisely: British Petroleum, Royal Dutch-Shell, and the Deutsche Bank. In 1914 these three companies formed the Turkish Petroleum Company, and began negotiations for the rights to develop Iraqi oil reserves. Local rulers were relatively autonomous by this time but still weak. They were therefore happy to trade the rights to this subterranean mineral of unknown value (to them) for hard cash. The outbreak of World War I forced a slight modification in Europe's commercial and colonizing efforts. Germany's defeat in the war resulted in its exclusion from the company, and Britain took control of its shares. Britain also landed a military force from India. They took over control of Basra and Baghdad provinces by 1917, claiming they were not planning to stay; they only wanted to help the Iraqis get rid of their unpopular rulers.

European colonial competition proceeded unabated during the war. Britain had sought Arab cooperation in the war, knowing they were increasingly unhappy under Ottoman Turkish rule.

Arab leaders had been agitating for independence, both from the Turks and the Europeans who had gained dominance in Arab lands despite Turkish rule. Debate often centered on strategy: Should they work for reform of the Ottoman system and greater autonomy, or for full independence? If they chose independence, should they struggle against the foreigners first and then the Turks, or vice versa? An offer of British assistance against the Turks seemed risky but worthwhile. It had come from British administrators in Egypt to the leading family of Mecca – the Hashemites, descendants of Prophet Muhammad ("sharifs") and traditionally in charge of Islam's two holiest cities, Mecca and Medina. The British knew that the Turks had been modernizing, largely with German help. They realized that in the impending war, the Turks – notoriously skilled warriors – would no doubt ally with Germany against the British, French, and Russians. They therefore looked for a way to weaken Turkish forces. Exploiting Arab discontent with Turkish rule, the British offered to recognize Arab independence in all liberated territories, in return for the Arabs' assistance in the war. They were to rebel against the Turks, effectively opening a second front in the war and preventing the Turks from providing significant assistance to Britain. This was a lot to ask, given that the Ottomans were not only the political rulers of the Middle East but also technically the spiritual leaders of the Muslim world. It was a momentous decision; among the earliest rules established in Islamic law was the prohibition of collaborating with non-Muslims against Muslim rulers. Nevertheless, after consultation with regional leaders, the Hashemite leaders decided to trust the Europeans. That, as it turned out, was a colossal mistake.

Along with the famous Lawrence of Arabia – the British officer assigned to work with the Arabs, the Arabs fought the Turks in the Middle East. They thus undoubtedly assisted in the defeat of the Germans and their allies. But after the war, instead of granting the Arabs independence as promised, the Europeans distributed Arab territories among themselves. This was what they had agreed secretly to do, at the same time they were publicly promising the Arabs independence.[1] In the secret Sykes–Picot Agreement (1916), France was designated "protector" of Arab Syria and Kurdish Mosul province. Britain would "protect" Baghdad and Basra provinces, and the Palestinian portion of traditional Syria, including what would be called Transjordan (the land on the eastern side of the Jordan River, all the way to Iraq). (Russia's claims, for example that the West Bank of the Jordan River, from Gaza to Tyre, should be international, were ignored as a result of the 1917 Bolshevik Revolution.) The treaties ending World War I established the independent state of Turkey, but ignored the promises made to the Arabs. Instead, they imposed the provisions of the Sykes–Picot Agreement, changing only the term "protectorate" to "mandate." But France now wanted a share of the company that was exploiting Iraqi petroleum resources. So France traded Mosul to Britain in exchange for defeated Germany's share in the Turkish Petroleum Company. (Later, the United States demanded inclusion in the deal. So in 1928 the Exxon, Mobil, and Gulf petroleum companies were incorporated into the company, and it was renamed the Iraqi Petroleum Company.)

Now Britain could put together Iraq: Mosul was added to Baghdad and Basra provinces to form the country. But what about a leader? The idea of the mandates was that the Europeans were supposed to watch out for the interests of the countries they were assigned, helping them along until they were ready to assume independence. They were not supposed to be colonial overlords. So Britain and France had to find Arab leaders they considered suitable for their new countries. Fortunately for them, there was a family of leaders available for work: the Hashemites. Their betrayal at the hands of the Europeans left them with only their domains in western Arabia. (Around this time the Saudi family began to expand from its realms in central Arabia, to which it had been limited since Egypt's Mehmed Ali had driven it back from Iraq. They would eventually defeat the Hashemites and name all of Arabia after themselves.) The sons of the elderly Sharif Hussein vigorously protested the violation of the Arab trust by the British. Faisal went north to Syria and set up a government in Damascus. But when he refused to accept the French mandate, he was forced out of Syria. Meanwhile, the Iraqis were rebelling against their British overlords. So the British offered the deposed Faisal the title of king of Iraq. He accepted, but only if the British changed their "mandate over" to "alliance with" Iraq, and with the concurrence of the Iraqi people (1922). Faisal finally had a throne, and Britain had a compliant Sunni Arab ruler for its very diverse but oil-rich Iraq.

According to the treaty of alliance, Iraq was technically independent, but Britain got to run the army and appoint advisors to run the economy and foreign policy. And the pernicious Capitulations were reasserted, exempting the British from local laws and taxes. The fact that Iraq was not, in fact, independent was made clear when, in 1932, the League of Nations recognized its independence. But even then, Britain maintained control of the economy and the military, and petroleum resources continued to be exploited by the foreign-controlled Iraqi Petroleum Company. Throughout this time, political opponents of the British-dominated monarchy were jailed, exiled, or executed, and insurrections were mercilessly suppressed. Perhaps most notoriously, Kurdish rebels in the early 1920s were suppressed with poison gas, and Shii uprisings resulted in the bombing of their villages. Foreign control of Iraq was not actually ended until a violent revolution in 1958.

The betrayal of the Arabs by the British and French resulted in the creation of other new states as well. Sharif Hussein and his son Faisal, when they were still in charge of western Arabia and Syria respectively (1918), decided to split Transjordan, that southern portion of traditional Syria situated between the West Bank of the Jordan River and Iraq. But after Faisal's defeat in Syria and transfer to Iraq, Britain decided to offer the rule of Transjordan to Faisal's brother Abdullah, provided he accepted their ultimate control, of course. Jordan got nominal independence in 1946 but, typically, Britain maintained control of the economy, military, and foreign policy. In 1955 the sovereign kingdom of Jordan was admitted to the United Nations, but real independence came only with the departure of British military leaders in 1956.

As noted above, traditional Syria included Lebanon, as well. Its mountains had separated it geographically from the rest of Syria and its long coast had opened it to cultural influences that had given the region a unique identity since the days of the ancient Phoenicians. Its strong local leaders had near-autonomy under Ottoman rule, but Lebanon was included in the French mandate over Syria. Under French control, the region was reorganized into a separate government, with a slight Christian majority. The government got its own constitution but, like Syria, was still controlled by France. Christian-dominated Lebanon was particularly pro-French; the language of administration and education was French, and the French dominated the economy. When France fell to Nazi forces during World War II, Lebanon and Syria were occupied by Vichy (pro-Nazi French) administrators. British and Free French troops defeated them and declared Lebanon and Syria independent, and promised the locals the right to choose between separate countries or a united Syria. But, in fact, French administrators remained. In 1943, contending Lebanese factions agreed on a National Pact; the Muslims would accept a Lebanon independent of Syria, provided the Christians would commit to a Lebanon independent of France. The agreement was not put in writing, and no census was taken, but it was accepted that the president of Lebanon would always be a Maronite Christian, the prime minister would be a Sunni Muslim, and the speaker of the National Assembly would be a Shii Muslim. Emigration of wealthy Christians to better economic fields abroad, and immigration of Sunni Muslims escaping war in Palestine/Israel would shift the demographic balance, severely straining communal relations in Lebanon.

The last portion of traditional Syria was given to Britain to rule, and it remains the most problematic place in the region: Palestine. The League of Nations granted Britain full control of the area in 1922, and included the Balfour Declaration within the mandate. The Balfour Declaration had been issued in 1917 by the British foreign secretary (Arthur James Balfour) in response to requests by Zionist leaders for British support for their movement. In view of centuries of Christian persecution of Jews, leaders of the World Zionist Organization had given up hope that European Christians would ever allow Jews to live in peace and security, with equal civil and political rights. They therefore wanted to establish a homeland for Jews in Palestine, as the ancient Jewish homeland had been called by Romans (after the name of its "Philistine" inhabitants). Lord Balfour wrote that the British government looks "with favour [on] the establishment in Palestine of a national home for the Jewish people and will use their best endeavours to facilitate the achievement of this object, it being clearly understood that nothing shall be done which may prejudice the civil and religious rights of existing non-Jewish communities in Palestine, or the rights and political status enjoyed by Jews in any other country."[2] Under British control of Palestine, the Jewish population increased exponentially, as Jews sought escape from growing anti-Semitism in Europe. According to Ottoman statistics, there were around 24,000 Jews in Palestine in 1882. By 1914, there were some 60,000. The British census in 1922 recorded 83,790 Jews, about 11 percent of the population. Within nine years, that number had increased to 174,610.[3] Arab leaders supported limited Jewish immigration on humanitarian grounds, but having been betrayed by the British and lost their autonomy in their own homelands, they were bewildered that Britain now decided to distribute these lands to Europeans.

As Nazism grew in Europe, threatening the very survival of the Jewish people, more and more European Jews immigrated to Palestine. Native Palestinians began to rebel against this mass immigration into their land. Zionist activists in Palestine became anxious to evict the British and form a sovereign state. The British mandate authorities in Palestine thus faced Arab uprisings against increased foreign immigration, and Zionist terrorism against both Arab opponents and the British presence. The pressure on Britain became too much, especially with their economy at home devastated by World War II. By the late 1940s, the British had to give up their troublesome colonial holdings. They made plans to leave not only India but Palestine as well. As they had in the case of India, they handed the problem of Palestine to the United Nations. And as they had done in India, the United Nations decided to partition Palestine. There were to be two states, one for Jews and one for Arabs, with the Jewish state receiving 55 percent of the land. The partition plan was rejected by the people whose land was being partitioned, of

Plate 5   The Dome of the Rock (687–91) in Jerusalem. © Sheila Blair and Jonathan Bloom.

course, but it was passed anyway. Immediately Zionist leaders declared Israel a state (May 15, 1948), and Arab leaders declared war. The Arabs were no match for the zealous European refugees. As a result of their defeat, some 800,000 Palestinians became refugees. Today, two wars (1967 and 1973) and countless United Nations resolutions later, Palestinians remain stateless.

Effects of Colonialism: The Challenge of Islamic Reform

The cumulative effects of colonialism were enormous. The sense of betrayal and humiliation was succinctly expressed by Ayatollah Khomeini, the leader of Iran's Islamic Revolution in 1979: "The government has sold our independence, reduced us to the level of a colony, and made the Muslim nation of Iran seem more backward than savages in the eyes of the world!"[4] Interestingly, Iran is among the few countries that had avoided direct colonial control. Nevertheless, its modern history is defined by the same kinds of commercial concessions and colonial competition (in this case, between Britain and Russia) that led to such disastrous results for other Islamic states.

Iran's first oil concession was granted in 1901, giving the right to exploit all of Iran's petroleum and natural gas for sixty years to the founder of British Petroleum (originally called the Anglo-Persian Oil Company, then the Anglo-Iranian Oil Company; it became British Petroleum [BP] in 1954) – in return for a cash payment of twenty thousand pounds, a relatively small annual fee, and less than one-fifth of the annual profits.[5] At that time the Qajar family dominated Iran. They had already sold the rights to develop Iran's tobacco to a British firm. That had caused a major protest in the 1890s, but the Qajars were undeterred. They were intent on modernizing the country, inviting Europeans to build telegraphs and railroads, establish a banking system, and modernize the bureaucracy and the army. Oil revenues had not yet begun to flow, so the Qajars were forced to rely on foreign loans to finance their projects. Protests among the Iranians against growing foreign influence increased. Despite their confiscation of religious properties, the Qajars could stop neither the clergy-led protests against their policies nor the country's growing subjugation to foreign powers. Protests turned into revolution in 1906. The British intervened and the Qajar shah (king) was forced to establish a constitutional government. But Russia intervened to strengthen the shah, lest the new government assert too much independence and reject Russian influence on the government. But with the Bolshevik overthrow of the Russian czars, Britain became the dominant foreign influence over the Qajars. Opposition increased and again turned into revolution. The Qajars were overthrown by a man from the modernized military, Reza Shah Pahlavi (1925).

The new king was intent on continuing modernization according to Western standards, but maintaining independence from foreign powers. He decided to take control of Iran's oil production, but a British fleet of warships and the League of Nations convinced him to simply accept a higher percentage of profits in the company. With the increased profits, the shah was able to increase the rate of industrialization, which often meant forcing new lifestyles on people who were perfectly comfortable with their traditional lives. Nomads were forced to adapt to settled life, and people who had always been farmers found themselves living in towns, or moved to different agricultural areas to make way for new industrial developments. The shah even banned traditional Iranian clothing, insisting that men wear European-style hats and women remove their veils. Opponents to these probably well-intentioned but over-zealous plans were ruthlessly suppressed. As the shah's popularity at home waned, his fascination with fascism increased, leading to conflict with the Allied powers. During World War I, America, Britain, and the Soviet Union agreed to occupy the country and depose the shah. In his place they put his son, Muhammad Reza Pahlavi. The new shah agreed to be compliant with Western interests, and the Westerners agreed to withdraw their troops from the country (1942).

Following World War II, Muhammad Reza Shah continued industrialization and modernization of Iran, with the same results as his father's policies. British Petroleum maintained sole control of petroleum production in Iran, and its revenues were so high that the portion paid to the Shah of Iran made him enormously wealthy and allowed him free reign in his country. But the rapid pace of change and introduction of foreign practices continued to result in social confusion and unrest. Protest, whether voiced by religious or secular leaders, brought severe repercussions. By 1950, Iranians became anxious to end the shah's undemocratic regime and gain control of their own resources. In 1951 the Iranian parliament, led by Muhammad Mosaddeq, called for nationalization of Iran's petroleum industry. The popularity of this policy led to Mosaddeq being named prime minister and the shah seeking exile outside the country. The Iranian government offered to buy out BP, including an offer to compensate them for a certain amount of future revenues. BP refused. They led a boycott of Iranian oil, and the United States' Central Intelligence Agency (with British support) then led a coup that ousted the nationalist government and reinstated the shah. BP then opened Iranian oilfields to other companies, including American ones and the National Iranian Oil Company, which would receive half the profits from Iranian oil.

From that time on, America gradually increased its influence in Iran, replacing Soviet and British influence. As a result, the shah's continued modernization, financed by ever-increasing wealth, became associated with American influence. As opposition grew, so did the shah's intolerance. Extra-judicial arrests, imprisonment, and torture at the hands of the dreaded secret police, SAVAK, were common. Rumors of tens of thousands of deaths by torture were no doubt exaggerated, but they were effective in spreading fear and loathing of the regime. Yet the shah's popularity in America increased. He was interviewed sympathetically on American television and was named one of Mr. Blackwell's "best dressed men," along with several Hollywood figures. The final straw was perhaps a symbolic one. On a western holiday (New Year's Eve 1977), the shah was toasted by an American president (Jimmy Carter) as an enlightened monarch who enjoys his people's confidence. In 1979 the shah was overthrown in the Islamic Revolution.

What this story demonstrates is that added to the humiliation and sense of betrayal was the frustration of colonized people's hopes for true independence and empowerment. In addition, the Muslim world experienced a leadership crisis. Not only was there a backlash against traditional leaders who had advised trusting in Europe in the first place, but the region lost many qualified people through emigration of the wealthier and better educated classes to regions where they could exercise greater independence. Military governments often took the place of civilian leadership, resulting from the fact that force was required to evict colonial powers. But ultimately the military governments were no more popular than the colonial governments. As a result, formerly colonized countries often experienced increased militarism and totalitarianism as they protested against their own dictators. At the same time, poverty deepened as colonized and formerly colonized peoples struggled in a fiercely competitive world market, at the cost of self-sufficient traditional economies. This typically led to rapid urbanization: mass migration of rural people into cities in search of work. But work was often unavailable, leading to growing unemployment and under-employment. The migration to cities also led to the breakdown of traditional family structures as males left home to find employment and women were forced into single-parenthood. Males unable to fulfill traditional roles as protectors and providers often experienced shame and despair, while women – burdened with running the family alone – began to question their traditionally sub-servient roles.

Thus economic, political, and social crises are the cumulative effect of colonialism in the Muslim world, as elsewhere. These effects have influenced developments in the Muslim world since the end of the nineteenth century. Since that time, the challenge facing Muslims has been to understand how their society plunged from the heights of affluence and influence, culture and learning in the Middle Ages to the depths of subjugation and despair, and then figure out what to do about it. But it would be a mistake to think that reform in the Muslim world began solely as a reaction to colonialism. In fact, voices of reform began to be heard as early as the fourteenth century. Nearly a century before Ibn Khaldun discussed the cycles of political life, another thinker living in strife-torn Mamluk times discussed challenges facing the Muslim community – the famous legal thinker Ibn Taymiyya (d. 1328).

Ibn Taymiyya believed that many of the problems of the Muslim world during his time resulted from leaders' efforts to keep the Muslim world politically unified. Ideally, he said, the community is united, but in reality it is divided into regional units. But lack of political unity need not compromise the strength of Islamic society, because that strength is based on shared moral commitment rather than on political leadership. The entire Muslim community can be morally united, cooperating through-out history to carry out God's revealed will, regardless of time or place. Differences of language, ethnicity, and culture pale in light of shared commitment to Islamic principles. Although Arabs have the advantage over non-Arabs in that their native language is Arabic, the language of the Quran, all believers are equal in the eyes of God. Ethnic and cultural diversity are part of God's plan, as the Quran confirms (49:13). Living in the wake of Christian and Mongol invasions, Ibn Taymiyya was very distrustful of non-Muslims. Still, he insisted on religious freedom and security for Jews and Christians, in accordance with the Quran. To do otherwise would violate the very purpose of the Islamic state: to establish justice. Like Ibn Khaldun, he believed that the goal of all revelation is to guide human beings in the struggle to establish justice and prohibit oppression. And that is a task in which all Muslims must cooperate.

Themes of Islamic Reform: Personal Initiative and Social Solidarity

In discussing this goal, Ibn Taymiyya brought up two issues that would become major themes of modern Islamic reform. The first is rejection of fatalism, passivity in the face of injustice, and relying on the intercession of saints rather than taking responsibility in one's society. Ibn Taymiyya argued forcefully against determinism, the idea that human beings have no free will. Through a unique series of arguments, determinism had actually become the dominant position among Muslim theologians by the time of Ibn Taymiyya. As noted, in Islam as in Judaism, there is greater emphasis in daily life on correct action than on correct belief. The basis of Islam was, as it remains, commitment to absolute monotheism. God is one and undivided in the Islamic perspective, absolute, all-knowing and all-powerful, our merciful creator and judge, from whom we came and to whom we must return. Acceptance of this ultimate reality is considered to be the basis of submission (*islam*). That submission will manifest itself in obedience or correct behavior which, in turn, will result in a just and peaceful society in which the well-being of even the weakest members is the measure of success. In other words, Muslims' primary concern is with actualizing God's will, rather than defining or categorizing beliefs. Nevertheless, challenges to belief did arise from time to time, and scholars had to formulate responses. In the process, scholars developed a set of beliefs that became part of official Islamic teaching.

One such challenge came from the Kharijis. The Kharijis ("Seceders") were religious zealots who had supported Ali, Prophet Muhammad's cousin and son-in-law and thus closest surviving male relative, as the legitimate caliph in his dispute with the dynastic Umayyads. But the Kharijis had turned against Ali when he agreed to arbitration in his dispute with his opponents. They saw this decision on Ali's part as compromise with evil. They believed the Umayyads sought leadership of the community out of sheer greed. To the Kharijis, this was a betrayal of Islam, meaning that Ali himself and all his supporters, in their compromise with people whose behavior violated Islamic norms, ceased to be true Muslims. They were convinced that true Islam/ *islam* can only be manifested in correct behavior. Someone who acts unjustly cannot be considered Muslim because a *muslim* is someone who does the will of God. They took literally the Quran's directive that "[t]ruth comes from your Lord, so let anyone who wishes to, believe; and let anyone who wishes to, disbelieve." (Quran 18:29) To the Kharijis this indicated ultimate individual responsibility, not only for belief but also for actions. If people behave badly, then, it is their own choice and therefore their own responsibility. At the same time, the Kharijis believed, it is the responsibility of the righteous to make sure those who are causing problems be stopped. They believed that the community had to be vigilant against those who did not live up to the Islamic model and undermined the goal of establishing a just society. They believed it was especially important that Muslims rise up against an unjust leader. They therefore continued to fight Ali, forcing him into a battle (658) in which most of them were killed. The rest escaped to remote areas and carried out sporadic attacks against rulers they believed acted in ways unbecoming a true Muslim.

Unfortunately, it is difficult to maintain social order based on a model of human perfection, and that is how the Khariji model looked to the majority of Muslims. The issue was particularly significant since excommunication had become a very serious matter in Islam. The Quran insists that "[t]here is no compulsion in religion." (2:256) It stresses that a plurality of religious communities is part of the divine plan. "If your Lord had so willed, he would have made mankind one community, but they continue to be divided." (11:118) "For each of you [religious communities: Jews, Christians, Muslims] we have established a law and a way. If God had willed it, He could have made you all one community. But [He has not] so that He may test you in what He has given you. So compete with one another in good deeds." (5:48) This acceptance of religious diversity and freedom was reinforced when Prophet Muhammad established the constitution for the various tribes of Medina, some Muslim and some Jewish. "The Jews . . . are a community along with the believers. To the Jews their religion and to the Muslims theirs."[6] Accordingly, as we saw, religious pluralism was a basic feature of Islamic societies and, in fact, a source of much of its strength and dynamism.

However, the matter of apostasy – rejecting Islam after having accepted it – was something different. As the Islamic community developed in history, belonging or not belonging to the community became a political matter. A Muslim was someone who accepted not only the word and will of God, but also the chosen leader of the community. Thus, anyone who turned against the leader of the community was considered a traitor, a threat to the well-being of the rest of the community. As in medieval Europe, people believed that everyone who accepted a particular religion had to be part of the same political community. Like premodern Europeans, the early Muslim leaders believed that anyone who rejected their leadership was declaring himself an enemy. As a result, they made the decision to force the rebellious tribes to submit to their leadership or face death.

This decision became a precedent in Islamic law. From that time on, the charge of apostasy was a grave matter. So when the Kharijis began labeling professed Muslims as apostates, it had to be taken seriously. After significant debates, the majority of

Muslims asserted their commitment to the Quran's emphasis on divine mercy and forgiveness. They stressed the struggle for social justice and the need to do good works, but chose to leave judgment of individuals to God. In a characteristic verse the Quran claims, "God lets anyone he wishes go astray and guides whomever he wishes." (35:8) To most Muslims this meant – as it still does – that only God can judge people's souls. If someone claims to be Muslim, the community must accept that. They have no right to declare a professed Muslim as an apostate based on the person's actions. Only God can judge the sincerity of a believer's heart. This majority position was developed by religious scholars (*ulama'*) as a theory of divine judgment based on mercy and forgiveness. They were known as Murjiis ("Postponers"), claiming that if people identify themselves as Muslims, others must accept them as Muslims. In legal codes, the position was expressed by Abu Hanifa, who claimed that no one can judge a professed Muslim to be a non-Muslim based on his/her behavior.

The practical implications of this view were obvious. Khariji-style radicalism was marginalized, their rebellions were put down, and people could once again live in peace and security. But acceptance of this position had other implications in society. After accepting the position that only God can judge people, some scholars concluded that the Umayyads' victory in the battles against Ali and the Kharijis was itself an expression of God's will. Since God is all-powerful, nothing can happen without God's will. Therefore, if the Umayyads are in power, that must be the will of God and people should not fight it.

This position may have resulted in political stability, but it also led to an attitude of fatalism about what happens in society. Scholars continued to raise the question of people's moral responsibility. A central feature of the Quran's teaching is that people will be judged by God based on their actions. They will be rewarded for good choices and punished for bad ones. But if God has pre-determined everything, including people's individual choices, then what about moral responsibility? What can we make of God's mercy and compassion if He is going to reward or punish people for doing things over which they really do not have control? In other words, what about free will? Muslims found themselves face to face with the age-old question of how to reconcile the notion of God's omnipotence (all-powerfulness) with human responsibility. This discussion gave rise to another school of thought among Islamic religious scholars, the Mutazilis. Known as Islam's rationalists, the Mutazilis chose to stress God's justice, rather than God's omnipotence. God revealed that He is just, and that He will judge people based on their choices. Therefore, we must assume that human beings have moral responsibility. But other scholars found this position offensive. They believed that the Mutazili position put boundaries on God, as if to say that God would be forced to judge in specific ways based on what human beings did.

There were many other issues involved in the scholars' discussions about the question of God's omnipotence and justice. But eventually the rationalist position was overruled, and the position of an anti-rationalist scholar, al-Ashari (d. 935), became official teaching. The Ashari rejection of excessive rationalism in religion became associated with fatalism and determinism. It was this that Ibn Taymiyya argued against. He found it particularly evident in Sufi mysticism, with its emphasis on personal enlightenment, rather than social issues. He considered determinism worse than heresy, because it makes a mockery of God's promises of reward for good behavior and punishment for evil. Ibn Taymiyya was not opposed to Sufis' emphasis on spirituality, but he rejected some practices associated with Sufism, such as praying to saints rather than relying on God. He urged instead personal initiative, and group cooperation in the struggle to create and maintain a just society. He was, in fact, an inspiration in this regard to the Wahhabis, although the Wahhabis would take the position further, rejecting Sufism altogether.

We saw in Chapter 3 that this theme arose again in seventeenth-century India, where Sufism was most dominant, with the reform movement of Sheikh Ahmad Sirhindi. Sirhindi was particularly concerned with the kind of Sufi teaching that undermined the significance of everyday reality. According to some Sufi thinkers, all reality is One, and external appearances are just illusions. Through meditation and other spiritual practices, people should rise above appearances and focus on the oneness of all reality. Sirhindi believed this attitude distracted people from commitment to following the law. Later, another Indian reformer, Shah Wali Allah of Delhi (d. 1762), taught that Sufis must purify their practice and conform to mainstream Islamic teaching in order to achieve the goals of a strong, just and united Islamic society.

Themes of Islamic Reform: Ijtihad

The second major theme of Islamic reform stressed by Ibn Taymiyya is the need to keep Islamic law flexible through ijtihad. As noted in Chapter 1, Islamic law is the core of Islamic society. Because of Islam's emphasis on good works and creation of a just society, concern with behavior is dominant, rather than concern with belief. True belief is assumed an essential pre-requisite to righteous behavior, but rational discussion of belief remained relatively marginal in Islam, as noted above. For that reason, the focus of religious thought in the first several centuries of Islam was law. By the tenth century, four major schools of Sunni law had been established, and a fifth developed in Shii Islam. During the early years of Islam, Islamic law was open and flexible. Its goal was to provide ongoing guidance for the ever-expanding Islamic community regarding what was permissible in view of the Quran and the example set by Prophet Muhammad. Flexibility was especially important, given that the Muslim world quickly came to include multiple, diverse cultures. In addition, circumstances rarely remained static; new conditions arise as societies develop economically, culturally, and politically. Yet by the tenth century, Islamic law began to lose its flexibility. The interpretive element of Islamic law is called *ijtihad*. Sometimes called "intellectual jihad," since the two terms share a single root (meaning "to struggle"), ijtihad was the means by which scholars derived legislation concerning new or changed circumstances from the sources: the Quran and the Sunna. But as we saw in Chapter 2, eventually the scholars added another source of Islamic law: consensus (*ijma*) among the scholars concerning the legal implications of the Quran and the Sunna. And using that source, they determined that no new ijtihad would be needed.

There is no particular date for this decision, nor is any one person given credit for it. The agreement that "the gate of ijtihad is closed" seems to have developed gradually. But it was evident by the beginning of the tenth century, says historian of Islamic law Joseph Schacht:

> [T]he point had been reached when the scholars of all schools felt that all essential questions had been thoroughly discussed and finally settled, and a consensus gradually established itself to the effect that from that time onwards no one might be deemed to have the necessary qualifications for independent reasoning [ijtihad] in law, and that all future activity would have to be confined to the explanation, application, and, at the most, interpretation of the doctrine as it had been laid down once and for all.[7]

In place of independent reasoning as a means for developing Islamic law to changing circumstances, imitation of precedent (*taqlid*) was recommended.

Presumably, the goal of the scholars in discouraging ijtihad and encouraging taqlid was to maintain continuity of Islamic law, particularly during the perilous years when the central power of the caliph was giving way to autonomous regional powers (see Chapter 3). But in the view of many reformers, the cessation of ijtihad makes Islamic law inflexible and unable to deal effectively with change. This had a number of negative results. First, it allowed Islamic law to be marginalized. Political authorities began to legislate independent of the legal scholars, to suit their own needs. As we saw, Suleiman the Magnificent was known as Suleiman the Lawgiver at home, because of his penchant for legislation. But his law was not based on the Islamic sources; it was not called Shariah. Suleiman's law was *qanun*, civil law as opposed to religious law. This pattern was followed by many other regional rulers, and especially by the European colonial powers. As non-Muslims, European citizens were exempt from Islamic personal law, and the Capitulations made them exempt from Islamic civil law. When European powers took control of Islamic governments, they continued the process of marginalizing Islamic law, setting up their own systems of economic, commercial, and civil law.

A related consequence of ending ijtihad was that people were left without religious guidance on new developments as they arose. In classical times, Islamic legal scholars (*fuqaha'*) were the bulwark of civil society. They were the people's protection against the autocratic tendencies of the caliph or sultan. Religious authority was the only protection against the sultan's awesome power. But the less flexible Shariah scholars were, the more people turned to secular law for guidance. By the modern era, religious law was restricted to ritual and personal matters – prayer, fasting, pilgrimage, charity, marriage, divorce, and inheritance. Shariah was considered a closed set. If Muslims wanted guidance on other matters, they would have to seek elsewhere.

Ibn Taymiyya recognized the danger of this trend even in the fourteenth century. He argued that ijtihad must remain active, lest Islamic law become irrelevant. Even during his day, the tendency was to consider Islamic law as a closed code, rather than a dynamic process of deriving guidance for human life from divinely revealed sources. For this reason, Ibn Taymiyya stressed the difference between Shariah and *fiqh*. Shariah is God's will for humanity, revealed in nature, in history, in the Torah and the Gospels, but revealed most perfectly in the Quran and the example set by Prophet Muhammad (the Sunna). It is eternal and changeless, and many specific regulations have been made explicit in it. These include regulations concerning ritual, some dietary restrictions, and major moral issues such as murder, theft, and usury. But human beings must use reason to derive legislation from the revealed sources for circumstances not specifically dealt with in revelation. The regulations derived in this way by human beings are fiqh, and they are not changeless or infallible. Ibn Taymiyya was appalled that people equated fiqh with Shariah. "Indeed, some of them think that Shariah is the name given to the judge's decisions; many of them even do not make a distinction between a learned judge, an ignorant judge and an unjust judge. Worse still, people tend to regard any decrees of a ruler as Shariah, while sometimes undoubtedly the truth (*haqiqah*) is actually contrary to the decree of the ruler."[8] In other words, Muslims in every generation must continue to seek guidance from the revealed sources, rather than rely on decisions made by people in the past. Not only are people fallible, so that their interpretations must be reexamined in light of new evidence or circumstances, but the fact that a decision was suitable for a given time and place does not necessarily mean it will remain suitable for all times and places. Ibn Taymiyya therefore insisted that ijtihad was a religious duty, essential to the vitality of the Muslim community.

The call to renew ijtihad was echoed by Muhammad Ibn Abd al-Wahhab, founder of the Wahhabis, in the eighteenth century. He treated Sufi saint worship and other innovations from early Islamic practice as the result of following human beings' guidance (*taqlid*), rather than that of revelation. Several other scholars during the eighteenth and nineteenth centuries echoed the same theme, but the most articulate expression came from Egyptian scholar Muhammad Abduh (d. 1905). In his view, taqlid was equivalent to intellectual servitude. He says that the Quran:

> forbids us to be slavishly credulous and for our stimulus points [to] the moral of peoples who simply followed their fathers with the complacent satisfaction and were finally involved in an utter collapse of their beliefs and their own disappearance as a community. Well it is said that traditionalism can have evil consequences as well as good and may occasion loss as well as conduce gain. It is a deceptive thing, and though it may be pardoned in an animal, is scarcely seemly in man.[9]

It was the creativity of ijtihad that had allowed the Islamic community to thrive, responding dynamically to changing historic circumstances and, within a few centuries after the death of Prophet Muhammad, to become one of the world's major political and cultural forces. But when people began to simply imitate their ancestors, elevating tradition to the status of virtue, they lost their initiative and fell into obscurity. They became easy prey for more energetic forces.

Unfortunately, at the same time that Abduh and other Islamic reformers were advocating reform of Islamic law and life through ijtihad, European powers were in the process of imposing European law codes in their newly acquired territories. They found it very difficult to deal with Islamic legal codes, particularly in conducting their international financial transactions. Criticizing Islamic law as rigid and archaic, they simply bypassed it. Thus, in the context of increasing foreign domination, many people became defensive of traditional law. It was essential to their identity as Muslims. Ultimately, it became difficult to distinguish between Western attacks on Islamic law as inadequate and Islamic reformers' critiques on Islamic law as moribund. As a result, many traditional Islamic scholars denounced reformers such as Abduh as "westernizers," trying to make Islam conform to European standards. (It is this complex interplay of historic forces that led to Islamic fundamentalism. We will discuss this further in Chapter 5.)

Themes of Islamic Reform: Commitment to Learning

The call for ijtihad is closely associated to another aspect of Islamic reform, the call for revival of Islam's intellectual strength. This became a third major theme of Islamic reform. It is based on recognition that Muslims had lost their commitment to learning. Among the first voices of this theme was Abduh's mentor, the famous Persian anti-imperialist Jamal al-Din al-Afghani (d. 1897). One of the things that annoyed Islamic reformers the most about European imperialism was the fact that it was often rationalized on the basis of claims that Islamic culture was backward and unscientific. Afghani reminded his listeners that it was Islam's commitment to learning that had produced the highest scientific culture in the Middle Ages. Scholars in the Muslim world had pulled together the ancient traditions of Greece, Egypt, Mesopotamia, India, and China, revising and developing them, and then transmitted them to Europe. Where would modern Europe be without Arabic numerals and algebra, for example? This is the way science works, he noted. It "is continually changing capitals. Sometimes it has moved from East to West, and other times from West to East." Science does not belong to any single culture; it is a world heritage to which various communities have contributed at various times. Muslims have made major contributions to science, as history demonstrates, and so the Europeans are mistaken when they claim that Islam is inherently unscientific or backward. In fact, he says, of all the major religions, Islam is the most supportive of science. When Islam came to the Arabs, they had no science. But Islam encouraged study and the acquisition of knowledge, and that's why they quickly developed the highest degree of learning known to the Western world.

However, Afghani also recognized that Muslims had lost their commitment to learning. They had lost the scientific spirit. In fact, they had passed it on to the Europeans and, he believed, that is why the Muslim world had been overcome by the Europeans. Afghani was particularly critical of religious scholars who opposed science. He said that their minds were actually "full of every superstition and vanity." They were unable to even take care of their communities, but they were nevertheless "proud of their own foolishness." These scholars are "like a very narrow wick on top of which is a very small flame that neither lights its surroundings nor gives light to others." And then Afghani points out the fallacy of their position. He says they have mistakenly "divided science into two parts. One they call Muslim science, and one European science." Having lost their commitment to learning, Muslim scholars did not even recognize their own scientific heritage when confronted with it in modern form. They thought it was all foreign. Similar to the way legal scholars had rejected their own reformers, accusing them of engaging in "westernization," religious scholars had rejected modern learning as "un-Islamic." He concludes, "[T]hose who forbid science and knowledge in the belief that they are safeguarding the Islamic religion are really the enemies of that religion. The Islamic religion is the closest of religions to science and knowledge, and there is no incompatibility between science and knowledge and the foundation of the Islamic faith."[10]

Abduh related the need for reform of Islamic law through ijtihad to Islam's inherent rationality. He described the rationality of the universe as a reflection of divine unity. Rejecting the tendency to split the world into the spiritual (religious) realm and the physical (non-religious) realm, Abduh insisted that the divine is revealed through all creation. That is why the Quran frequently reminds people to examine the world and see the signs of God in it. Based on the Quranic command to "read the signs" and "seek knowledge," Abduh actually considered the exercise of reason to be essential to the practice of Islam, even a form of worship. Failure to exercise one's reason was a religious failing: "So the Quran directs us, enjoining rational procedure and intellectual enquiry into the manifestations of the universe, and, as far as may be, into its particulars, so as to come by certainty in respect of the things to which it guides."[11]

Conclusion

Islamic reformers in this period agreed that there is no distinction between religious and secular science. As Ibn Khaldun had pointed out five hundred years earlier, human beings were created with reason; that is the difference between them and animals. They were then commissioned by God to use it in order to carry out the "trust," their divinely mandated task to create and maintain a just society. Whether scrutinizing revelation, history, or nature, reason is required on an ongoing basis. When Muslim scholars lost their commitment to careful reasoning, relying instead on the past and making a virtue of imitating it, the Muslim world began to lose its cutting edge. It fell into stagnation and became easy prey for foreign adventurers. Among the most eloquent expressions of this theme is found in the work of Indian reformer Muhammad Iqbal (d. 1938). Iqbal said that Islam had fallen into stagnation five hundred years ago, when it substituted inertia for Islam's essential dynamism and adaptability. Also an advocate of ijtihad as the key to Islam's ability to adapt to ever-changing circumstances, Iqbal also found its root in human rationality. He criticized the scholars for their conservatism and fear of change. Although deeply mystical himself, he also criticized Sufis for excessive concern with the inner meanings of things. Muslims must be concerned with the practical world. Like Ibn Khaldun, Iqbal also criticized those who take a passive attitude toward life, waiting for God to send a great man to lead the community properly. In Ibn Khaldun's case, it was the Mahdi that people were waiting for; in Iqbal's critique, it was the *mujaddid*, or renewer (someone God would send at the beginning of every century to guide people, a belief Iqbal traces to the sixteenth century). Relating the exercise of reason again to ijtihad, he said the "closing of the door of ijtihad is pure fiction" resulting from "intellectual laziness . . . If some of the later doctors have upheld this fiction, modern Islam is not bound by this voluntary surrender of intellectual independence."[12]

Muhammad Iqbal – the advocate of dynamic, adaptable, progressive Islam, is known as the father of Pakistan. But today Pakistan is one of the poorest nations in the world, with an illiteracy rate of nearly two-thirds, and is ruled by a military dictator. It is also one of the most conservative states in the Muslim world. And Pakistan is just one example. The Muslim world overall has made little progress toward its goals in the modern era. What happened to the movement to revive Islam's commitment to reason and progress, which had been developing for centuries? Is it still alive anywhere? These are the questions that will be addressed in Chapter 5.

Chapter 5

Obstacles and Prospects for Islamic Reform

Reformers such as Afghani and Abduh viewed the superior strength of European culture as a temporary phenomenon. As we saw in Chapter 2, scholars in the Islamic world had developed the natural sciences to their highest level during the Middle Ages. Muslim mathematicians, astronomers, and physicians were among the world's most renowned scholars. But by the modern era, little evidence of this greatness remained beyond some terminology that has become so familiar that it is hardly associated with Islam anymore. Reformers were convinced that Islam's eclipse had resulted from Muslims' dereliction of duty and violation of their own principles. Muslims had fallen into a comfortable traditionalism, following the paths of their ancestors rather than forging new paths and meeting new challenges with confidence. As discussed in the previous chapter, early modern reformers criticized three areas of Islamic life in which this was particularly evident: Sufi practices that resulted in passivity and superstition, the practice of taqlid (following precedent) among legal scholars rather than ijtihad (independent reasoning), and the rejection of modern learning by religious scholars. As a remedy, many reformers called for the renewal of Muslims' commitment to learning and science. Jamal al-Din al-Afghani insisted that science was not just a luxury; it was the basis of power. "If someone looks deeply into the question, he will see that science rules the world." He recounted the stories of the Chaldeans, the Egyptians, the Phoenicians, and the Greeks, and concluded, "The Europeans have now put their hands on every part of the world . . . In reality this usurpation, aggression, and conquest has not come from the French or the English. Rather it is science that everywhere manifests its greatness and power. Ignorance had no alternative to prostrating itself humbly before science and acknowledging its submission."[1]

The inevitable question arises: Why has Islam's long tradition of reform not resulted in the desired renaissance? The term "renaissance" or "rebirth" (*nahdah*) was, in fact, optimistically used in the nineteenth and twentieth centuries to describe the goal of both cultural and religious reform movements. As late as 1989 a Tunisian Islamic reform movement renamed itself to the Renaissance Party (*Hizb al-Nahdah*). Now, in the wake of September 11, the fall of the Taliban and the fall of Saddam Hussein, the Islamic recovery seems more distant than ever. In this chapter we will discuss what obstacles have impeded the progress of Islamic reform, and survey the prospects for success.

Obstacles to Islamic Reform

Islam's traditional commitment to learning was undermined when the great medieval empires began to fade, chiefly because of the way traditional Islamic education developed. Although sciences continued to flourish in the Muslim world well into the sixteenth century, they did so generally under the patronage of wealthy sponsors. Scientific study was not institutionalized as part of Islamic education. It was left to private scholars under the patronage of wealthy sultans and princes. The natural sciences sometimes produced unorthodox speculation, such as the possibility of the eternity of the world and the impossibility of the resurrection of a dead body. As a result, religious scholars spurned such studies and, as we saw in Ibn Taymiyya's fourteenth-century critiques, limited their own studies to what had already been done. They dwelt on complex discussions of the Quran's grammar and inimitable style, and of the ancestors' commentaries on the Quran's grammar, style, and meaning.

In the twentieth century, reformers often focused on this phenomenon. They expressed deep concern that reverence for tradition, combined with a distaste for controversy, effectively precluded innovation in Islamic education. During Europe's "Dark Ages," Muslim religious scholars' lack of science did not appear to be a problem, and early reformers' critiques fell on deaf ears. But when the medieval Islamic empires fell into decline, they were no longer able to subsidize the sciences at their private institutes. At the same time, European scholars began to develop the very sciences they had inherited from the Muslim world. European colonization of the Muslim world made it very clear that the tables had turned. Muslim reformers again recognized the need for reform. If the Muslim world had produced the world's cultural leaders in the past, so the reformers argued, it could do so again. It was simply a matter of recovering Islam's lost dynamism and commitment to learning in the service of humanity.

Unfortunately, once European colonialism began, the reform process was compromised. Islamic religious scholars may indeed have fallen into an inflexible traditionalism. But they remained the backbone of Islamic society, the symbol of Islamic identity. And that symbolic value increased proportionately with every step European powers made in the Muslim world. Colonial control brought European innovations into the streets of the capitals – automobiles, highways, telephones and telegraphs, European clothing, music, and public mixing of sexes. The greater the displacement of traditional lifestyles by these developments, the more important symbols of tradition became to the majority of people under the European yoke. The religious scholars may have been old-fashioned patriarchs but the majority of colonized people felt that they were *their* old-fashioned patriarchs. For their part, the traditional religious scholars had become quite accustomed to the status quo. True, a good percentage of their traditional financial support had been confiscated by the newfangled states. But the scholars still enjoyed the status of respected elders in society and undoubtedly felt a responsibility to their communities. In this context, the more Islamic reformers criticized the traditional scholars as impediments to development and independence in the Muslim world, the more they sounded like the Europeans who justified their imperialism by claiming the Muslims were incapable of running their own affairs. As a result, many Islamic reformers, in fact, alienated people in their own societies. In the eyes of people already under the extreme pressure of colonization, these internal criticisms – despite their good intentions – seemed to be betrayals. Not all religious scholars rejected reform, of course. But tradition was well entrenched. Muhammad Abduh could not even get his own university – the famous center of Sunni Islamic learning, al-Azhar University, to teach Ibn Khaldun's *Muqaddimah*. "It would be against the tradition of teaching at al-Azhar," he was told.[2]

The case of nineteenth-century Egyptian reformer Qasim Amin is a good example. Amin joined in an ongoing debate about the need for reform in the status of women. Abduh, like other reformers, had insisted on the need for educational reform in the Muslim world. Also like other reformers, he added that women as well as men must be educated. The education of both sexes was essential to social development. At the same time, several reformers added, Muslims must reexamine their overall treatment of women. They must recognize that in many ways the standards of dignity and equality established by the Quran had been abandoned in the case of women. This was the theme developed by Qasim Amin. In a book called *The Liberation of*

Woman (*Tahrir al-Mar'a*, 1899), he argued that women's education and improved status in marriage, including ending the seclusion of women behind veils or at home, was a necessary component of the overall health of Islamic society. But Amin's criticisms took the form of an attack on traditional religious scholars. He said the religious scholars have absolutely no interest in science. They can discuss the grammar of a single phrase from the Quran "in no fewer than a thousand ways," he said, but if you ask them anything about history, geography, or science, "they shrug their shoulders, contemptuous of the question . . . ." Amin then concluded that the religious scholars are not only greedy but lazy.[3] This, combined with sarcastic descriptions of how unattractive traditional Egyptian women are, naturally turned people against his reforms. His criticisms of Islamic society sounded just like the criticisms leveled by the Europeans. For a large part of the population, these criticisms led to intensification of traditionalism. For many people, as for the religious scholars themselves, the issue at stake had changed. It was no longer a question of the need for reform but a matter of loyalty. To conform to demands for reform appeared to be collaboration with the imperial enemies. And this was exactly how Amin was attacked. Dozens of extremely hostile articles appeared in the newly developing Egyptian press. Some even accused Amin of carrying out his "attacks against Egypt" under orders from the British colonial government. Even now he is described as an unrepentant Westernizer – in effect, a "self-hating Muslim." The reforms he urged were not revolutionary. Many others before him had called for improvement in the status of women, in accordance with Quranic standards. But now, because of the association of such critiques with the foreigners who had taken control of their world, opposition to Islamic reformers took the form of defending traditional practices. In other words, calls for reform in the context of colonialism often had an effect that was the direct opposite of what was intended. They increased people's attachment to tradition.

A similar phenomenon occurred in Pakistan, perhaps a more chilling example of how Islamic reform efforts were thwarted in the context of colonial and post-colonial politics. Pakistan was created in 1947 when Britain partitioned India. It is one of the two states in the world established for a single religious group (the other one is, of course, Israel, created when Britain partitioned Palestine in the same year). It was to be an Islamic state, ruled by Islamic law. The idea of Pakistan was developed by the progressive reformer Muhammad Iqbal (see Chapter 4) in the 1930s. On the level of practical politics, however, the cause of Pakistan had been taken up by the real father of Pakistan, Mohammad Ali Jinnah (d. 1948), still known today as the "Great Leader" (Qaid-i Azam). Jinnah was a highly sophisticated man, trained in law in England. When he returned to India he became a successful attorney and active in the independence movement, working with people like Jawaharlal Nehru in the Congress Party (Indian National Congress Party) and Iqbal in the Muslim League to free India of British control. His original goal was for a united, democratic India. He was known as the "ambassador of Hindu–Muslim unity." His orientation shifted, however, when elections in British India in 1937 resulted in Hindu governments that excluded Muslims from provincial cabinets. This convinced Jinnah that Muslims, even in a democratic India, would be utterly marginalized. He therefore adopted the call for a separate Muslim state, becoming leader of the Muslim League. But his vision for Muslim Pakistan was a progressive one, where there would be no religious test for citizenship. It was to be a secular democracy, where people of all faiths could live in freedom and equality. Within this ideal Islamic state, all people would be free to develop and contribute constructively to world culture.

The vision for Pakistan was, in fact, a template for a modern Islamic state which should be consulted by those involved in the ongoing debate about Islam and democracy. Some contemporary scholars claim that Islam is inherently authoritarian and therefore incompatible with democracy. They often cite as evidence claims made by some traditional Muslims that "popular sovereignty" violates the Islamic principle that God is the ultimate sovereign and lawgiver, and the lack of working democracies in the Muslim world today. But Jinnah's vision for Pakistan – the vision that inspired the mass following that proved an unstoppable force even for imperial Britain – was clearly democratic.

Jinnah was elected the first president of the Constituent Assembly of Pakistan, which met August 10, 1947 to begin the process of forming a government and constitution. He died before that process was completed, without expressing a preference for parliamentary over presidential democracy. But there is no doubt that Jinnah insisted on constitutional democracy. When he became Pakistan's first governor-general upon the state's creation August 15, 1947, Jinnah broke with imperial tradition. Instead of pledging allegiance to the British monarch, he vowed to "bear true allegiance to the Constitution."[4] In speeches to the Constituent Assembly, he stressed pluralism and popular sovereignty as the critical elements in the new state:

> If you ... work together in a spirit that every one of you, no matter to what community he belongs, no matter what relations he had with you in the past, no matter what is his colour, caste or creed, is first, second, and last a citizen of this State with equal rights, privileges and obligations, there will be no end to the progress you will make ... My guiding principle will be justice and complete impartiality, and I am sure that with your support and cooperation, I can look forward to Pakistan becoming one of the greatest Nations of the world.[5]

Jinnah and his followers agreed that these principles reflected essential Islamic values, and that their democratic government would always be guided by Islamic principles. According to the Objectives Resolution passed in 1949, which has survived through the ups and down of successive Pakistani governments, Pakistan will be a democratic state whose power is exercised "through the chosen representatives of the people." This power is delegated by God to the people based on popular sovereignty and Islamic principles. Those principles are "democracy, freedom, equality, tolerance and social justice," as well as an independent judiciary.[6]

The mass popularity of Jinnah's plan combined with Jinnah's effective leadership convinced Britain to agree to an independent Pakistan. However, the state was inherently unstable, divided by over 1,000 miles between East and West Pakistan, and covering populations of widely divergent geographic regions, differing languages and cultures; deprived of the industrial infrastructure that had developed in India; and in some cases even left without control of their own water resources. These conditions created overwhelming challenges for the new state's leadership. The ideals of an enlightened Islamic society – nurturing human dignity, committed to learning, acting as a positive force for peace and social development – were utterly overwhelmed by the struggle to maintain stability under increasingly difficult circumstances.

Pakistan's military, organized by the British, was the most stable institution in the country, and they naturally stepped into the breach. By 1958 martial law had been imposed. A constitutional government had been established in 1956; a second constitution was adopted in 1962, and a third in 1973. But instability continued, including wars with India over the disputed territory of Kashmir and the 1971 civil war that resulted in East Pakistan's transformation into the independent state of Bangladesh. The result of this instability was recurrent suspension of democracy and imposition of martial law. Islam – as represented by the traditional religious scholars – was the one thing held in common by the entire population (except for small minorities of Christians, Hindus, and Parsis). Therefore, it formed the natural counterweight to the military.

The first period of martial law was declared during extreme tension among various factions, including those in East and West Pakistan. The military ruler, General Mohammd Ayub Khan, tried to bring stability through economic development and a government that was better suited to Pakistan's diverse needs. Part of the latter effort included the establishment of the Islamic Research Institute. Its responsibility was to develop Islamic legislation suitable for a modern state. Qualified scholars would examine traditional Islamic legal codes and recommend ijtihad in cases in which circumstances had changed and traditional legislation no longer was suitable for the goals of the Muslim community. By the mid-1960s, Pakistan had implemented a number of the institute's recommendations, including some reforms of traditional statutes. For example, the medieval law limiting the legitimacy of women's testimony in court was revised in accordance with Quranic teaching on human equality and recognition of the change in women's social status through education. Polygyny (the right to marry more than one wife) was also limited, and the medieval equation of *riba*, which was forbidden by the Quran, with any level of interest whatsoever, was revised. According to the new interpretation, *riba* was identified as usurious interest rates, which continued to be forbidden, while reasonable interest rates were determined to be permissible in order to allow Pakistan to participate in the global economy.

Although Ayub Khan's economic policies were initially successful, poverty and instability quickly returned and, with them, opposition to Ayub's policies. Ayub Khan responded to the opposition with greater autocracy. As political unrest escalated, people turned again to traditional religious leaders for solace. The traditional religious leaders, in turn, asserted their prerogative over Islamic legislation. Among their first victims was the director of the Islamic Research Institute, Fazlur Rahman. The "modernist" legislation he had advocated was characterized as un-Islamic by the conservative Muslim leaders whose methods Fazlur Rahman had criticized. As he summarized his arguments later, Rahman had said that Islamic education had grown stagnant and unresponsive to the needs of society. He said that rather than participating in ijtihad, scholars simply memorized texts and then argued about details of what they had memorized. This "fruitless ingenuity" was a "waste of valuable intellectual energies." The scholars could reproduce traditional commentaries on the Quran in all kinds of ingenious ways. For example, they might write their commentaries while limiting themselves to only those letters of the alphabet that had no diacriticals (like the dot on the letter "i" or cross on the letter "t"), requiring them to use only about half of the letters of the alphabet. And they could write commentaries on traditional commentaries "where, by reading words horizontally or vertically or in some cases diagonally, in each case successively or alternately (or by reading lines and not words alternately) on each page, one simultaneously obtains readable texts of as many as five disciplines (say, grammar, theology, law, logic, and philosophy) and in as many as three languages – Arabic, Turkish (Ottoman), and Persian!"[7] But they could not produce legislation that would allow Islamic society to develop intellectually, socially, economically, or politically.

Fazlur Rahman's exasperation with the traditional scholars was interpreted as an insult to Islam. Despite the fact that he was a very devout Muslim, traditional scholars accused him of being anti-Islamic. Even today, the reforms he initiated as director of the Islamic Research Institute have been described as giving "a veneer of Islamization" to secular government. Fazlur Rahman was accused of participating in anti-religious activity, and went into exile in 1968.[8] Since that time, Pakistan has experienced a debilitating cycle of civilian governments, internal and regional conflict, and martial law. Successive governments have sought legitimacy through Islam, allowing traditional religious scholars authority over social issues. As a result, by the 1980s virtually all the legal reforms of the 1960s were struck down. Women's legal testimony was again limited, efforts were made to forbid all charging or paying of interest, and certain other high-profile "Islamic" legislation was enacted. Pakistan today is a military dictatorship yet again.

The dynamic at work in these two cases is clear. The Islamic world had been deprived of its independence and resources by foreign powers who justified their actions by disparaging the cultures and abilities of the people they control. In this context, the reform movement that had been developing long before foreign domination began, was stifled. Traditional religious scholars became the symbols of all that is sacred and secure in society. Calls for reform by Muslim activists became almost indistinguishable from the contempt of foreign rulers. Islamic reformers could be, and often were, accused of un-Islamic or anti-Islamic behavior, even collaboration with the enemy. In the aftermath of independence, this pattern became more complex. Traditional scholars became – in addition to being symbols of all that is sacred and secure in society – symbols of political legitimacy. As noted above (Chapter 4), foreign powers rarely left their lucrative colonial holdings voluntarily. They often had to be forced out by military rebellions, leaving military rebels in control of the newly independent countries. We also saw that the boundaries of these newly independent countries were frequently imposed by the departing powers. In many cases they violated traditional boundaries, grouping together people who had little in common (as in Iraq and Pakistan) and separating people who were used to being together (as in Syria, Lebanon, and Jordan). These two factors made traditional religious scholars even more important. The traditional Islam they represented was often the only thing shared in common by diverse populations, and their stamp of approval could grant legitimacy to even the most non-traditional government.

This is just what happened in Pakistan. As the country's economic, social, and political problems mounted, successive governments found themselves catering to religious figures calling for stricter adherence to Islamic law, a process called "Islamization." One of the major proponents of Islamization was the Jamaat-i Islami, a group founded in 1941 by Abu'l Ala Mawdudi (d. 1979). The Jamaat-i Islami is often called an Islamic reform group since Mawdudi called for renewal of Islamic society through ijtihad. (The terms "Islamist" and "political Islam" are generally used by scholars for such groups.) Mawdudi said that all Muslims have the right to participate in legislation in an Islamic state, not just the economic or religious elite. He rejected the term "democracy" in favor of "theo-democracy," since all legislation must conform with revelation, but he believed that legislation in an Islamic state must remain flexible and responsive to the needs of society.[9] But in fact the reforms advocated by the Jamaat-i Islami have not been directed toward Islamic law as such. They leave the traditional codes generally intact, instead calling for changes in the government. And because of their emotional appeal within society at large, they have been able to bring pressure on Pakistan's various governments. Neither the Jamaat-i Islami nor similar, smaller religious parties have been successful in federal elections. Until 2002, they never received more than 4 percent of the vote. But as governments become less and less effective in dealing with real economic and political problems, and therefore less and less popular, the religious parties have been able to pressure successive governments into more and more emphasis on traditional Islamic legislation.

This "Islamization" trend has been particularly evident since the 1980s, when General Zia al-Haq was in charge of Pakistan. A military dictator and close friend of the United States, Zia relied on his Islamic credentials for legitimacy. It was his regime that revoked most of the reforms of the 1960s. Successive governments followed suit. In 1991, the "Enforcement of Shariah Act" was passed, reiterating that "Islam has been declared to be the state religion of Pakistan and it is obligatory for all Muslims to follow the Injunctions of the Holy Quran and the Sunnah . . ."

Expressing the no doubt sincere faith of millions of Muslims, the act simply concludes that Islamization will result in the elimination of "bribery, corruption, obscenity, vulgarity, social evils, false amputations, etc."[10]

The problems that continue to challenge Pakistan are institutional, structural, and multi-dimensional. With a population of nearly 150 million, two-thirds illiteracy rate, staggering foreign debt, extraordinary instability in neighboring Afghanistan and Kashmir, and the constant nuclear threat from India, it is not surprising that Pakistan has not had the leisure to develop an effective democratic political culture in its brief history. However, the government's continued reliance on the appeal of Islamization for legitimacy, in lieu of practical programs for good governance and economic development, has had a negative impact on Pakistan's efforts to develop democracy. Nawaz Sharif, for example, was the prime minister deposed and exiled under charges of corruption by the current leader of Pakistan, General Pervez Musharraf. To the extent that Nawaz was able to maintain popularity, he did so by appealing to Islamization. At the same time, he actually undermined some basic elements of democracy, such as the freedom of elected representatives to vote according to their consciences or the will of their constituents. Under Nawaz, Amendment 14 was passed, requiring that elected representatives vote with their parties or lose their elected seats, with no protest from the religious parties.

Even though the religious parties have been unable to bring real reform to Pakistan, they have been able to pressure governments by bringing people into the streets for demonstrations. This pressure is then used to secure further concessions from the government. For example, in the Spring of 2000 Chief Executive General Pervez Musharraf attempted to revise the "Blasphemy Law" (Provision 295-C of the Constitution), which allows anyone accused of insulting Islam to be jailed. According to this law, which was passed during Gen. Zia al-Haq's

Islamization program, anyone found guilty of any sort of insult to Islam or Prophet Muhammad is subject to the death penalty. For the most part, the law has been used against minorities, primarily the minority Ahmadi sect and Christians. Many Pakistanis oppose the law, believing it is simply a tool used to silence people and therefore a violation of the principles of an Islamic state. Nevertheless, the religious parties brought "street" pressure against Gen. Musharraf's efforts to revise the law, in the form of mass demonstrations, and the government was forced to back down.

These concessions do have the effect of empowering people who otherwise feel disenfranchised from the power politics. But the appeal is emotional only. The concessions give a sense of power, but no real power measurable in practical terms – for example, no more efficient government, no better infrastructure, no clean water or sewage treatment plants, no better education to allow greater economic competitiveness, no power to bring about changes that would improve their standard of living or that of future generations.

In fact, the longer economic, social, and real political development are put off, the more potent this emotional appeal becomes to those sectors of society without access to economic power or the intellectual or educational apparatus to figure out how to get it. As a result, Pakistan has been caught in a "catch 22." Those who advocate effective political reform are silenced, often by the very people suffering from lack of good governance. Without good governance, radicalization increases. Even before September 11, many people were expressing fear of "Talibanization" in Pakistan, where a growing number of rural male students – those with minimal modern education – were being drawn to an even more conservative blend of hostility toward "the West" combined with an ultra-traditional social outlook. Like Afghanistan's Taliban (see below), they believe that "Islam" – practiced purely and simply and thus bringing the favor of God

– was able to drive the Soviets from Afghanistan, and then to overthrow the corrupt warlords who succeeded them. Unconcerned about the economic or social conditions in Talibani Afghanistan, they call for even greater "Islamization" as the answer to Pakistan's problems. The BBC reported from Peshawar in the Spring (April 10) of 2001, for example, that some 200,000 men had gathered for an international conference of the conservative Deoband school. According to the report,

> Conference organizers have demanded the expulsion of what they call Christian and Jewish forces from the Arabian peninsula . . . The organizers said they want Muslim youth to be prepared to fight a war there. The call was echoed in a statement sent by . . . Osama bin Laden from his hide-out in neighbouring Afghanistan . . . and the group want their interpretations of Islamic law enforced in Pakistan.[11]

Even among students receiving higher education, there is growing radicalization, as evidenced in increased use of the Blasphemy Law against professed Muslims. In a recent case, a professor at the Homeopathic Medical College in Islamabad was accused by his students of insulting Prophet Muhammad. In response to a question about circumcision, Mohammad Younas Sheikh pointed out that the Prophet Muhammad's tribe did not practice circumcision. Since male circumcision is considered essential to Islam (although it is not mentioned in the Quran), some students perceived this response as an insult to the Prophet and invoked the Blasphemy Law. The professor was found guilty and awaits execution in a Rawalpindi jail.

For many Muslims, this represents a violation of everything Islam stands for. The professor is a devout Muslim who believes authentic Islam is a progressive force in society. In a letter written from his cell on death row, he described the "rising wave of aggressive ignorance" and "theocratic darkness" that is overtaking many people in Pakistan.[12] His view is shared by the majority of educated Muslims, including religious scholars; his defending attorney was himself a mullah (traditional religious scholar). But the trend toward radicalization is also real, and must be understood in context. On the one hand, it grows out of a popularization of the reform movement in Islam. The reformers described in the previous chapter were individuals, often operating from positions of intellectual authority (such as universities) and publishing their views for an educated audience. But in the 1920s, some Islamic reformers began to organize themselves into religio-political parties. Unlike the earlier political parties, generally populated by educated people from the cities, who had often gone to European schools and were generally comfortable with modern life, these newer religious parties represented the majority of people – still rural or newly urbanized and generally traditional in outlook. Motivating people to become politically active in order to achieve independence and good governance became a major task of the new Islamist parties. Competing with secular and military governments with far greater resources, often supplied through close relations with foreign powers, the Islamist parties demanded that foreign models of government be replaced with authentic Islamic governments. At the same time, radicalization represents increasing frustration with seemingly endlessly deferred progress. Amid deepening poverty and notoriously undemocratic governments, demands for independence, good governance, and economic development became increasingly shrill.

In this context, a new kind of discourse in Islamic movements developed over the course of the twentieth century. In it, the self-scrutiny and critique that characterized earlier reformers' discourse were replaced with a defensiveness and tendency to blame all of Islamic societies' problems on the West. The rational analysis of early reform was likewise replaced with emotional accounts of the suffering caused by Western governments and their allies within the Muslim world, and utopian descriptions of what is generally characterized as "the Islamic solution." There is no need to turn to the outsider; Islam is sufficient for all human needs. This new discourse served the dual purpose of appealing to the broadest possible audience in largely under-educated populations, and motivating them to become politically involved. Thus, rather than criticizing people's passivity and superstitions, as the earlier reformers had done, the populist reformers focused on what could be called consciousness-raising. As in the American Civil Rights movement and certain quarters of feminism, listeners were regaled with accounts of the suffering they had undergone at the hands of a stereotyped enemy and encouraged to rise up and assert their rights. (Interestingly, in all three cases, the stereotyped enemy was usually the same: white men.) At the same time, the new populist discourse marked a subtle shift in the focus of modern Islamic movements, from reform to revival. Earlier Islamic activists had noted Islam's strength in the past and placed their calls for reform in that context; Muslims had to reform in order to recover the strength inherent in Islamic societies. The new trend in Islamic movements was not to deny the need for reform, but simply to stress the inherent glories of the religion as the means to recover Islamic societies' lost strength.

The first and still most widespread of these religio-political parties was the Muslim Brotherhood. It began in Egypt in the late 1920s and gradually spread throughout much of the Arabic-speaking world. Its founder, Hasan al-Banna (d. 1949), described his reasons for founding the Brotherhood with typical emotional appeal. He told of a group of laborers working for the British on the Suez Canal who came to him and begged him to lead them to freedom. According to al-Banna's account, they said:

> We are weary of this life of humiliation and restriction . . . [W]e see that Arabs and Muslims have no status and no dignity. They are no more than mere hirelings belonging to the foreigners . . . We are unable to perceive the road to action as you perceive it, or to know the path to the service of the fatherland [*watan*], the religion and the *ummah* [Muslim community] as you know

it . . . All that we desire now is to present you with all that we possess, to be acquitted by God of the responsibility, and for you to be responsible before him for us and for what we must do. If a group contracts with God sincerely that it live for his religion and die in his service, seeking only his satisfaction, then its worthiness will assure its success however small its numbers or weak its means.[13]

This is clearly an appeal to the emotions of his audience, allowing them to empathize with the suffering of the weak and lowly members of society. The appeal is then compounded by identifying the villain responsible for the tragic plight of these pathetic workers and, by extension, of the Muslim people as a whole. It is "the West." Like the Crusaders of yore, "[t]he West surely seeks to humiliate us, to occupy our lands and begin destroying Islam by annulling its laws and abolishing its traditions."[14] Whether it is capitalist Europe or communist Russia, al-Banna tells his listeners, the West is degenerate. The West's intellectual freedom and democracy are good, and there is nothing wrong with capitalism as such, al-Banna explains, but the West is hopelessly materialistic, always willing to oppress the poor for the sake of the wealthy. Similarly, communism's emphasis on social justice and solidarity is admirable, al-Banna says, especially by contrast to Europe's selfish individualism. But communism's atheism and tyranny (its "Red barbarism") are no better than czarist Russia's degenerate culture. Altogether, he concludes, Western ideologies have resulted in "a deadening of human sentiments and sympathies, and . . . the extinction of godly endeavors and spiritual values."[15] The solution to society's woes, then, is perfectly clear:

We believe the provisions of Islam and its teachings are all inclusive, encompassing the affairs of the people in this world and the hereafter. And those who think that these teachings are concerned only with the spiritual or ritualistic aspects are mistaken in this belief because Islam is a faith and a ritual, a nation and a nationalism, a religion and a state, spirit and deed, holy text and sword . . .[16]

The most popular ideologue of the Muslim Brotherhood, Sayyid Qutb (d. 1966), further developed the defensive and utopian themes of al-Banna. Like al-Banna, he explained that the world is divided between the two hostile blocs of communists and capitalists. Each of them is determined to control the world for its own benefit and with no thought for the well-being of anyone else. "[N]either the Eastern Bloc nor the Western Bloc gives any credence to the values they advocate, or consider us ourselves as of any consequence . . . . We will receive no mercy from either bloc. We are oppressed strangers in the ranks of both. We are therefore the tail end of the caravan regardless of the road we take."[17] To get right to the bottom of things, the West seeks to destroy Islam because they "are angered only because of the believers' faith, enraged only because of their belief."[18] The source of people's problems, then, is nothing less than the perennial struggle between good and evil, and the answer to all problems is clear. Islam "is capable of solving our basic problems, of granting us a comprehensive social justice, of restoring for us justice in government, in economics, in opportunities and in punishment . . . ." There is no need to turn to any other system.[19]

Anyone tempted to follow Western models only has to look at the misery in which Western people live. They walk around in "grief, sorrow and uneasiness. [Western man] is miserable, distressed and prey to confusion. He seeks to escape from life. Sometimes he takes refuge in opium, hasheesh and wine and sometimes wishes to forget his inner anxieties through the craze of rapidity and idiotic ventures. . . . It seems as if it were a hoard of demons who were chasing man and he were trying to flee and evade it, but it were always taking hold of his neck."[20] Obviously, then, people must avoid Western innovations. Islam is the only proper course for humanity. It is the "only path that grants man the excellence, bestows on him true freedom, and saves him from the curse of slavery." Islam, by granting sovereignty over human beings to no one but God, is the only religion that truly liberates humanity from earthly bonds.[21]

Sayyid Qutb remains the dominant spokesman of this emotional and defensive approach to Islamic revival. He was influenced by and influenced Abu'l Ala Mawdudi (d. 1979), the founder of South Asia's dominant movement of Islamic revival Jamaat-i Islam. In Mawdudi's works Islam is again the ideal solution to all of society's ills. Unlike other systems, says Mawdudi, Islam does not allow one group to dominate another. "In fact, it is an all-embracing order that wants to eliminate and to eradicate the other orders which are false and unjust, so as to replace them by a good order and a moderate program that is considered to be better for humanity than the others and to contain rescue from the illnesses of evil and tyranny, happiness and prosperity for the human race, both in this world and in the Hereafter."[22] Unlike Western secularism, Islam "is a complete scheme of life and an all-embracing social order where nothing is superfluous and nothing lacking."[23]

The effectiveness of this new stress on Islamic revival was never more apparent than in the impact of Iran's Ayatollah Khomeini. We saw in the previous chapter that Shah Muhammad Reza Pahlavi was returned to power after the American-led overthrow of the popular anti-shah prime minister Muhammed Mosaddeq in 1953. The shah then continued his efforts to strengthen central power and speed Iran's transition to a modern secular state. His White Revolution, launched in the 1960s, involved land redistribution shifting power from traditional landholders, modernization and secularization of schools, and increased women's rights. There was opposition from many – often conflicting – quarters, including communists and capitalists, intellectuals and peasants. But leadership of the opposition was taken by those with the broadest authority, religious scholars, and Ayatollah Khomeini quickly rose to the forefront.

The popular speeches of Ayatollah Khomeini reveal a similar pattern of motivational appeal. Like that of the founding ideologues of the Muslim Brotherhood and Jamaat-i Islami, the focal point of his discourse was justice for the suffering people of Islam. He often appealed to Shii heritage in ways designed to elicit emotions. In an address delivered after the shah's troops killed several students at a seminary in Qum, he reminded the audience of the deaths of women and children at the hands of the Umayyad rulers in the eighth century. Shii Muslims believe that the Umayyads were usurpers, and that the grandson of Prophet Muhammad, Hussein, was the rightful leader of all Muslims. But the Umayyads massacred Imam Hussein and his followers. Khomeini compared the shah's attack on the seminarians to that of the Umayyads against Hussein and his followers, arousing enormous emotion in the audience. He then described the attack as nothing less than an attack on Islam itself:

> What did [the Shah's regime] have against the students of theology? . . . What had our eighteen-year-old sayyid [a student who had been killed in the attack] done to the Shah? What had he done against the government? What had he done against the brutal regime of Iran? [The audience cries.] Therefore we must conclude that it wanted to do away with the foundation. It is against the foundation of Islam and the clergy. It does not want this foundation to exist. It does not want our youth and elders to exist.[24]

After capturing the sympathy of the audience, Khomeini typically shifted emotional gears, from pathos to anger. He focused the blame for the sufferings of Iranians on foreigners or on the shah's regime, described as merely a tool of foreigners. A typical example: "All of our troubles today are caused by America and Israel. Israel itself derives from America; these deputies and ministers that have been imposed upon us derive from America – they are all agents of America, for if they were not, they would rise up in protest."[25] Khomeini then directs the audience's anger, telling them to rise up against the "agents of the enemies of Islam" and expose the sinister and destructive designs of imperialism.[26]

The emotional appeal, the external focusing of anger, and the general call to action were all extremely effective in consciousness-raising. Building upon the work of his predecessors, such as Ali Shariati (d. 1977), Khomeini's skillful articulation of these themes ultimately resulted in a mass following. He was able to fill the streets of Iran's cities with hundreds of thousands of people protesting against the shah's regime. Ultimately, he was able to overthrow that regime in the Iranian Islamic Revolution of 1979.

The ability to clearly identify both a foreign source of all society's problems and a simple and sacred solution was no doubt more appealing than self-critical rational analyses calling for extensive internal reform advanced by scholars like Muhammad Abduh and Fazlur Rahman. It allowed a vent for the emotional energy aroused by the accounts of their own suffering. As noted, reformist themes were not eliminated from this discourse. Sayyid Qutb, for example, called for flexibility in Islamic governments, rather than a simple return to the past. He said, "The Islamic system has room for scores of models which are compatible with the natural growth of a society and the new needs of the contemporary age. . . ."[27] Government must be based on consultation, and there must be no discrimination based on ethnicity or gender.[28] Mawdudi was extremely conservative socially, believing women's place is in the home, obedient to her husband. He was also conservative politically, insisting that non-Muslims be excluded from Islamic governments. But even he expressed support for ijtihad in order to develop suitable legislation for modern societies. But reform is a long process, and reformers in the Muslim world face formidable odds at the outset. The majority of governments in the Muslim world are undemocratic. Most have some form of democratic institutions in place, but in most cases a strong military holds real power and little opposition is tolerated. The Islamic Revolution in Iran in 1979 was an apparent success, and it raised the hopes of Islamists everywhere. But it also raised the fears of governments throughout the Muslim world that they would be the next targets of Islamist reform. Suppression of Islamic political parties increased throughout the 1980s as a result. Suppression, in turn, intensified the emotionalism of Islamist rhetoric. In countries supported by the United States, heightened anti-Americanism was the inevitable outcome of the growing sense of victimization.

Indeed, as the twentieth century drew to a close and the Islamic Revolution in Iran receded into the past, there were no further victories of Islamist reform movements. Islamist parties made progress in some elections. In Algeria, for example, in 1991 the popular Islamic Salvation Front (*Jabhat al-Inqadh al-Islami*, in Arabic; usually known by its French initials, FIS) was poised to dominate in the first federal elections open to opposition parties since independence from France. But the military stepped in and stopped the elections, plunging Algeria into an ongoing bloody civil war.

At about the same time, the Soviets ended their twelve-year occupation of Afghanistan. The Afghan resistance was considered a legitimate war of self-defense. It was a legitimate form of jihad, and resistance fighters were known as the Mujahideen (plural form of the Arabic term for "holy warrior" or "one who fights jihad"). Many of their leaders took their inspiration from Islamist ideologues such as Hasan al-Banna, Sayyid Qutb, and Mawdudi. Their efforts were strongly supported by US weapons, training, and finance, but the victory was considered a victory for Islam, as was the subsequent disintegration of the Soviet Union. However, following the Soviet withdrawal, Afghanistan also fell into a brutal civil war. After tens of thousands of deaths, order was restored only by the Taliban. These were former refugees, many of them orphans who had grown up in camps in Afghanistan and Pakistan due to the devastation caused by Soviet occupation and the civil war.

The plight of all refugees of the war in Afghanistan was dire. The international community, especially America, had been very generous supporting the resistance to Soviet occupation. But America's interest in Afghanistan ceased following Soviet withdrawal. The refugees – numbering in the millions by the year 2000 – were left to the care of the already strained resources of the United Nations, host countries such as Pakistan and Iran, and non-governmental organizations. The Taliban gained their name ("students") because they were among the few refugees to receive any education at all. They received no modern education, only rudimentary religious education that was heavily influenced by puritanical tendencies similar to those of the Wahhabi Saudis, the source of much of the funding for this education. They became convinced that returning to the simplest lifestyle of early Islam, and strictly adhering to religious rules, would please God. In return, God would allow them victory over their enemies.

The Taliban set out to cleanse Afghanistan of what they considered non-Islamic practices. They were victorious in their native Kandahar, and received a great boost when they captured a massive weapons depot at nearby Spinboldak. With these armaments they were able to drive the warring factions northward and impose their strict rule throughout most of the country, capturing the capital Kabul in 1996. The relief of Afghanistan's population was at first palpable. After nearly two decades of war, the streets were once again safe to walk – provided one adhered to the Taliban's notoriously strict regulations. Women were removed from mixed company, men were forced to grow beards and pray regularly, alcohol and music and all graven images were destroyed – from American pornography to the massive Buddha sculptures that had stood at Bamiyan for sixteen centuries. But still prosperity did not appear. Despite being "students," these uneducated refugees were incapable of the demanding technical rebuilding that Afghanistan required. By the end of the 1990s their entire annual budget consisted of a few hundred million dollars, earned mainly by resale of surplus weaponry left over from Soviet occupation, smuggling of automobiles from the Gulf to Pakistan (avoiding Pakistan import duty), and heroin production. (The Taliban were opposed to drugs and attempted to stop cultivation of the opiate-producing poppies but the country was undergoing a drought, and poppies were their only drought-resistant crop.)

By the end of the twentieth century, therefore, Islamists looked in vain for further victories. Algeria and Afghanistan were particularly painful failures. But even Iran was struggling. The majority of its population had lived their entire lives under the Islamic regime. They had observed strict social regulation and enjoyed very few freedoms, but they saw little benefit in return. Iran was internationally isolated, economically stagnant, and social unrest was mounting. It therefore appeared that Islamism was at a crossroads. It could redouble its efforts, attempting to increase support for overthrowing un-Islamic governments and installing Islamic governments. We saw this kind of reaction in Pakistan, for example, in the phenomenon characterized as "Talibanization." For those influenced by Sayyid Qutb, Islamism can go beyond radical to outright militant. Qutb taught that the primary task of Muslims today is to "change the [prevailing unjust] condition and make it better." Muslims must "deliver blows at the political forces that make men the slaves of something that is not Allah. . . ." Qutb instructs his followers: "Kill every leader who looks for fame, wealth, power and social station. . . ." instead of Islamic purity.[29] A minute fraction of the world's Muslim population, the people influenced by this line of thought have been responsible for the terrorism that scars the name of Islam in the contemporary era. A far more prevalent reaction to the failure of Islamist movements in the late twentieth century is the development of more objective and practical reform efforts. This is the route Iran itself has taken.

Prospects for Islamic Reform

The Islamic government Ayatollah Khomeini called for was established by 1981. It was called the Islamic Republic, and was described as government by legal scholars (*velayat-e faqih*). It had an elected National Consultative Assembly, in accordance with the Quran's advice to Prophet Muhammad to consult with his followers, as well as an elected president. Religious scholars had to approve of candidates and their legislation, making sure it was in accordance with Islamic principles. This was a novel form of government, the first working model of an Islamic democracy. But the religious scholars in charge were generally from the revolutionary generation, still motivated by concern to protect Islam from the West, especially America. The fear of America was heightened by US support for Saddam Hussein in his eight-year war against Iran in the 1980s. The Iranians were well aware of the tyranny and brutality of Saddam's secular regime, and could only assume that it was hatred of Islam that motivated the USA to support him. Thus, religious officials generally maintained their single-minded commitment to a religio-moral righteousness, including strict social policies designed to protect people from Western-inspired decadence. But within twenty years of the Islamic Revolution, a new generation had grown up. Having been protected from Western decadence, they felt quite secure in their Islamic identity. But they still felt the need for reform within Islamic society, practical reforms that would allow them to develop and reintegrate into world culture. There was growing frustration with the isolation of the country and stagnation of the economy, and increasing discontent with the lack of personal freedoms among the populace. These feelings were expressed in the landslide election of Mohamed Khatami as president in 1997. Khatami focused on the need to establish what he calls a "new Iran," clearly appealing to popular sentiment.

Mohamed Khatami was elected on a platform of comprehensive reform in Iran. His election showed overwhelming approval of his plan to reintegrate Iran into the family of nations.[30] In order to achieve this goal, he said Islamic society overall must transform itself.[31] Despite continued efforts, Islamic societies have not achieved development. Muslims are still struggling economically, socially, and politically. Khatami acknowledges in his writings that the history of colonialism is a factor in this situation, but it is now up to Islamic society to deal with it effectively. Defensiveness and emotionalism, he says, are no help at all. Instead, Muslims must examine their own societies and find out what is necessary to remedy their problems. Khatami says that the first step is to develop the freedom of thought and expression necessary to carry out this analysis. "[T]ransformation and progress require thought," he says, "and thought only flourishes in an atmosphere of freedom. But our history has not allowed human character to grow and to be appreciated, and thus the basic human yearning for thinking and freedom has been unattended at best and negated at worst."[32] People must not just blindly follow their religious leaders, no matter how pious or brilliant they are, he says. They must develop their own intellects and knowledge in order to help guide society collectively. And they must be able to do so without fear of censorship or persecution.

In a radical departure from Islamist anti-Westernism, Khatami says that Muslims should learn from the West. Western history should serve as an example from which Muslims may choose what to emulate and what to avoid. There are positive strengths and achievements in Western society which Muslims should try to incorporate into their own societies. Again, breaking from Islamist patterns, Khatami says that modernity is not some godless rejection of religion, as many have portrayed it. Rather, it is a rejection of "autocratic and whimsical rulers" who plagued the pre-modern West and continue to plague the Muslim world. He insists that it takes freedom of thought and expression to cast off the shackles of these autocrats who base their legitimacy on traditional interpretations of religion.

True, Khatami says, the West is hedonistic and greedy, but that is not because of its freedoms. And materialism is actually weakening the West. Khatami thinks that Karl Marx was partly right about the West. He says Marx "was a great pathologist of the capitalist order," even if Marxism itself was "an impractical and unrealistic philosophy."[33] But that does not mean that everything about the West is bad or that everything about Islamic society is good. They are both flawed and can learn from each other.

Khatami is convinced that freedom, including intellectual freedom, is an essential Islamic value. For that reason, it is particularly offensive to him that freedom has been suppressed by some revolutionary leaders in the name of religion or even tradition. In fact, he says, we have to be careful about what we call tradition. The mere fact that something is old does not make it tradition. Nor does the fact that something is traditional make it good. The only "good traditions" are the immutable laws of God – what Khatami calls the "laws governing existence." Human beings make mistakes interpreting God's law, so no human tradition should be considered sacred. Human interpretation must always be distinguished from divine law, he says, and that requires intellectual freedom. Returning to the perennial themes of Islamic reform, Khatami concludes that lack of freedom has resulted in fatalism and excessive mysticism, distracting people from their communal responsibilities.

Once Islamic societies regain their freedom and intellectual momentum, they can work to develop into contributing members of the world community. But they cannot achieve their goals in a vacuum. The West must be constructively engaged, through "rationality and enlightenment," not fanaticism. Fanaticism merely harms Islam. Islamic societies do not need martyrs; they need what he calls "religious intellectuals," able to explore new options and develop new ways to deal with a world the traditional authorities could never have imagined.

Overall, Khatami's vision for Islamic societies is free and tolerant, reasonable and flexible, based on a holistic understanding of human beings. In other words, he envisions a society that meets both the material and spiritual needs of its citizens. In his inaugural address, he described the ideal society for Iran. Iran should be a society that respects "social and individual security within the framework of the Constitution." It should have "clearly defined rights and duties for citizens and the government." Its government should "officially recognize the rights of the people and the nation within the framework of law. . . ." Such a government needs "organized political parties, social associations, and an independent free press." This is a society "where the government belongs to the people and is the servant of the people, not their master, and is consequently responsible to the people."[34]

Islam at a Crossroads?

The path taken by Iran in electing Mohamed Khatami as president clearly represents a very hopeful trend in modern Islam. Its rational self-critique stands in stark contrast to the stridently defensive and militant stance taken by the Taliban and their supporters. Both trends exist in Islam today, often in uneasy balance. Moderate and progressive Muslims struggle against formidable odds. Progress toward reform is inevitably slow. Even in Iran, despite the popularity of reformist President Khatami, many Muslims express frustration with his inability to overcome the opposition of the traditionalist religious leaders and continue to agitate for a more open society. In the Fall of 2002, popular reformist scholar at Tehran University, Hashem Aghajari, became an overnight sensation when he argued for Islamic reformation. Insisting that Muslims go back to the scriptural sources, he said they must "separate historical Islam from essential Islam through analysis. . . ." Among the non-essential historical developments, he claimed, was the clergy itself. Unlike Sunni Islam, Shii Islam developed a hierarchy of scholars

recognized as the sole authorities in matters of religious interpretation. (The highest level is "ayatollah.") But Aghajari pointed
out that this rigid hierarchy only developed in the last century.
It is, therefore, not part of essential Islam. What is essential, he
claims, is that every Muslim "consider himself the direct recipient
of the Holy Book. . . . We have the right to receive and interpret
this message on our own and based on our own circumstances."
To simply follow what the clergy says is regressive, said Aghajari.
In fact, he said, it is "fundamentalist," and allows the clergy to
declare, "Anyone who is not with us is our enemy . . ." By contrast, Aghajari concluded, "Islamic Protestantism [reformist Islam]
is intellectual, practical and humane and as such is a progressive
religion. . . ."[35]

For his courage in confronting the traditionalist clergy, Aghajari
was condemned to death for blasphemy. However, mass demonstrations forced the conservatives to back down, encouraging
more scholars to speak out publicly for reform. They included
supporters of elderly reformist Ayatollah Hossein Ali Montazeri.
Ayatollah Montazeri was a senior cleric and the successor
Ayatollah Khomeini chose for himself. But in the late 1980s
Montazeri became critical of the Islamic government's ruthless suppression of its opponents. He was therefore replaced
as successor to Khomeini. In 1997 he was placed under house
arrest by Khomeini's successor Ayatollah Khamenei, for calling
for a more open government. Under enormous public pressure,
including a petition signed by over 100 members of the Iranian
parliament, Montazeri was released in early 2003. Although
he has not been given a public platform, his views continue
to circulate and increase in popularity via the Internet
(www.montazeri.com).

Even Ayatollah Khomeini's granddaughter Zahra Eshraghi,
sister-in-law of President Khatami, has publicly called for openness in Iran. She campaigned for President Khatami in 1997,
and currently works promoting women's rights in the Interior
Ministry. She rejects the veil, pointing out that people voluntarily

wore it as a symbol of revolution against the imperious shah. But when the Islamic government forced it upon women, its symbolism changed. "We have only ourselves to blame," she says, echoing both the self-critical attitude of contemporary reformers and their frustration with the slow pace of reform.[36]

In contrast to revolution, it is the nature of reform to be slow. Revolution is imposed from outside, by force; reform must come from within, voluntarily. The steps toward reform are incremental and so widely scattered as to sometimes go unnoticed, but they are being taken. In the Spring of 2003, for example, former President Rafsanjani joined the movement for ending Iran's social and political isolation, supporting a call for reopening relations with the United States. This, despite US President Bush's own claim that "if you're not with us, you're against us," and subsequent classification of Iran as part of a worldwide "axis of evil." As well, a major figure in Islam's most conservative state, Saudi Arabia, has endorsed the cause of reform. In early 2003 Crown Prince Abdullah proposed an "Arab Charter," calling for greater political participation and economic integration within the Arab world. The crown prince stops short of advocating democracy. Nor did the Arab and Islamic summit meetings in March 2003 endorse Abdullah's charter. Instead, delegates ended up in a shouting match over issues stemming from the US-led plan to invade Iraq. But Abdullah's plan did acknowledge that "lack of recourse" has been exploited by some people in ways that undermine the Arab interests, perhaps a reference to terrorists who exploit social unrest to serve their own agendas. It should be recalled that Osama bin Laden and many of his followers were Saudi citizens.

There are other hopeful signs of progress toward reform in the Muslim world. In Afghanistan, work is progressing toward a new government suitable to the needs of the Afghan people. Although there is still a great deal of anti-Americanism and traditionalism, some religious scholars are showing a willingness to undertake serious self-criticism in the effort to develop a society that truly expresses Islamic values. A senior religious scholar recently criticized the Taliban for not understanding or properly applying Islamic law. Another religious authority condemned the indiscriminate use of extreme punishments, such as amputation for theft and stoning for adultery, and called instead for efforts to develop a society in which people's needs are fully satisfied. In Indonesia, following the October 12, 2002 terrorist attack that killed nearly 200 people at a Bali nightclub, Islamic leaders supported a government crackdown on militant religious groups. Indonesia's two most popular religious organizations are the Nahdatul Ulama and the Muhammadiyyah. Leaders from both groups – including former Indonesian president Abdurrahman Wahid of the Nahdatul Ulama – condemned the nightclub attacks as terrorism. In the Fall of 2002, an Islamic party defeated Turkey's long-running secularist Republican People's Party. The Justice and Development Party (known by its Turkish initials, AKP) has a long history of challenging the military-supported secularists, only to find itself banned in a violation of democratic principles. But the popularity of its moderate platform, based on Islamic values of social justice, pluralism, and democracy, continued to grow. Following its unqualified victory in the November 2002 elections, it was allowed to form a government. It is currently working toward Turkey's long-term goal of inclusion in the European Union, and showing commitment toward progress in resolving ongoing human rights issues in Turkey.

Many other instances of progress toward human rights and democratization in Muslim countries could be cited, as well as some counter examples, such as indications of increased militant activity in Morocco and Bahrain. But should political developments really be taken as indicators of the nature of Islam? There are well over one billion Muslims in the world today, nearly one-fifth of the world's population. Roughly two-thirds of them live in countries that were colonized by Europeans and have been working for decades under severe economic and political conditions, following often brutal struggles for independence. Some are embroiled in history's most intractable conflicts, such as the fight to control the Holy Land. Others continue to struggle in the aftermath of "Great Power" conflicts, such as Afghanistan, or under unpopular governments that are none-theless supported by Western powers, such as Egypt and Saudi Arabia. Many Muslims find it extremely frustrating that their religion is judged on the basis of political developments in these countries. The vast majority of Muslims, like the majority of people everywhere, simply try to live their lives in accordance with their religious values, struggling with the challenges of everyday life. They have no say in what the governments of self-styled Islamic states do, much less what the terrorists do. Yet they find themselves increasingly judged by the actions of these newsmakers.

Indeed, among the most pressing concerns of Muslims today is how to deal with the Western world's disrespect for Islam. Some Muslims are convinced that Christians actually despise Islam and are determined to destroy it. This perception is a unique phenomenon. It is different from the very real concern of Jews about anti-Semitism. Christians have over the centuries tried to destroy Jews – in the Inquisitions, the pogroms, and the Holocaust. The target was not Judaism, however; Christianity incorporated Hebrew scriptures into its Bible, including its basic history and beliefs into Christian teaching. Christianity could hardly exist without the heritage of Judaism. Christians cannot ridicule Abraham or Moses, for example, without ridiculing their own heritage. Instead, Christians developed a fear and loathing of Jewish people. As a result, many Jews share the perfectly understandable conviction that Christians hate Jews. Ridicule of Jewish people is therefore a matter of grave concern.

The concern among many Muslims, however, is not that Christians hate Muslim people. Muslims themselves often make fun of Muslims. A good example is a quote that began to circulate in the early twentieth century: "The true nature of Islam is hidden from the world by a great wall of Muslims." But historical experiences have made Muslims extremely sensitive to ridicule of Islam, the religion, and its prophet Muhammad. From its earliest history, Islam found itself dismissed as a false religion brought by a false prophet. Many Jews and Christians became Muslim, of course, and many others lived in peaceful respect for the religion. But many rejected the teachings of Prophet Muhammad. The Quran even records that they were rejected as sorcery or trickery. As noted in Chapter 2, there is a long heritage of Christian lore extremely demeaning to Islam and Prophet Muhammad. The Crusades were launched in order to reclaim the Holy Land for Christianity from the Muslims, who were described as infidels – people with no true belief at all, rather than believers in a different religion. Colonial activity in the Muslim world was always associated with the work of missionaries, and was therefore easily incorporated into the pattern of Christianity's efforts to eradicate Islam. When author Salman Rusdhie, in his novel *The Satanic Verses* (1988), parodied Prophet Muhammad and his family in extremely insulting ways, the book was hailed as a masterpiece in England and America. This was taken as more evidence of the West's contempt for Islam and Muhammad, the prophet not simply revered but loved by Muslims everywhere. America's steadfast support for Israel despite its violation of United Nations Security Council resolutions concerning the rights of people who happen to be predominantly Muslims, and recent military campaigns against Afghanistan and Iraq, have likewise been interpreted as part of a campaign to destroy Islam.

That conviction has resulted in attacks against Christians in some parts of the Muslim world. In Pakistan – again, one of the poorest countries in the Islamic world, and one of the countries most deeply affected by America's policies in Afghanistan – churches have been attacked. In a particularly gruesome example, seven Pakistani Christians, working for a Christian charity in

Karachi, were murdered in the Fall of 2002. However, this radical reaction represents only a tiny minority of Muslims. The majority Muslim view was represented by the thousands who marched in the streets of Karachi condemning religious extremism. Kamal Shah, police chief of Sindh (the state in which Karachi is located), condemned the murders: "I would rate it as the most tragic terrorist incident since 9/11." The Catholic Archbishop of Karachi, Simeon Pereira, expressed his solidarity with Islam: "No real Pakistani Muslim would ever think of committing such a barbaric attack."[37]

In fact, the terrorist attacks on America on September 11, 2001, were committed by people convinced that the West intends to destroy Islam. Terrorist tracts invariably attempt to inflame emotions and recruit followers by recounting the suffering of Muslims at the hands of those who would destroy the religion. But again, the views of the majority of Muslims were represented in the unequivocal condemnations of terrorism by Islamic scholars around the world. The chief legal authority of Saudi Arabia (Grand Mufti Abd al-Aziz al-Shaykh) and the head of Cairo's al-Azhar University (Shaykh Muhammad Sayyid al-Tantawi), the center of Sunni Islamic learning, both issued fatwas (authoritative legal rulings) claiming the attacks were against Islamic law. Terrorizing the innocent is a gross and intolerable injustice, they claimed. Both targeting of civilians and suicide are violations of Islamic law. Muslim Brotherhood scholar Shaykh Yusuf al-Qaradawi, along with numerous other Islamic scholars around the world, characterized the attacks as *hirabah*, not jihad. Hirabah is a category of crime in Islamic law that includes attacks against society at large. It is the only crime in Islam that carries a mandatory death sentence.[38]

Nevertheless, the attacks confirmed the conviction of certain American evangelical Protestant preachers that Islam is a religion of violence. Derogatory statements about Islam ricocheted around the Muslim world with lightning speed. Rev. Franklin Graham, for example, called Islam "a very evil and wicked religion" on a news broadcast shortly after September 11. Rev. Jerry Vines, past president of the Southern Baptist Convention, was quoted describing Muhammad as a "demon-possessed pedophile." In an appearance on the television program "60 Minutes," Rev. Jerry Falwell described Prophet Muhammad as "a violent man, a man of war," concluding, "I think Muhammad was a terrorist." Within two weeks, Falwell realized his offense and issued an apology, saying, "I intended no disrespect to any sincere, law-abiding Muslim." Shaykh Tantawi in Cairo then issued a public statement accepting the apology. Shii scholar Ayatollah Hussein Mousavi Tabrizi agreed, stating that "a person courageous enough to apologize for his errors is worthy of praise. It's humanitarian and good Islamic behavior to accept an apology from a person who admits making a mistake."[39] Others issued statements vowing to reconsider their views, and President George W. Bush spoke out against those who misrepresent Islam as a terrorist religion and insult Prophet Muhammad. But the damage had been done. Riots broke out in India, resulting in a number of deaths, and anti-American sentiment clearly escalated in Pakistan. Within days after Falwell's statements, another statement was issued in the name of Osama bin Laden, attempting to convince Muslims not to be fooled; the West really seeks to destroy Islam. The statement referred to the US-led "crusade against the Islamic world," and urged Muslims to unite in order to "defend the targeted faith, the violated sanctity, the tarnished honor, the raped land and the robbed riches . . . [T]he Americans and the Jews . . . will not stop infringing upon us except through jihad."[40] And in elections held in Pakistan in October 2002, as noted above, for the first time in history religious parties received a plurality of votes, increasing their number of seats in parliament by a factor of ten. As one observer put it, many Pakistanis seemed to feel that a vote for the Islamist parties was a vote against America.[41]

The perception that Christians have no respect for Islam was intensified by the desecration of holy sites in Iraq during the second Gulf War. Sacred mosques were bombed, and the tomb of Abu Hanifa, founder of the oldest school of Islamic law, was raided. Countless artifacts and documents from some of the world's most ancient civilizations – Sumeria, Akkadia, Assyria, Babylonia – were lost. Included among them are examples of the world's earliest form of writing and religious relics. Undoubtedly most devastating, however, is the loss of sacred texts. Copies of the Quran dating from the first century of Islam had survived both the destruction of Baghdad in 1258 and Tamerlane's attacks in 1401. But they did not survive the American-led war in 2003. This made Rev. Franklin Graham's participation in a religious service at the Pentagon on the most solemn day of the Christian calendar, Good Friday (April 18, 2003), particularly painful for many Muslims.

Emotions continue to run high on both sides, and the situation remains volatile. The conciliatory public statements by evangelical Christians, President Bush, and Islamic scholars have been effective in most quarters. But resentment of the Christians' insults lingers, and terrorists will continue to try to exploit it for their own purposes.

Among the majority of Muslims, however, the far more common reaction to ongoing conflict and misrepresentations of Islam is increased effort to represent Islam in ways they believe are authentic. They deeply resent the "hijacking" not just of jets, but of Islam itself by terrorists and radicals. They reject the right of fanatics to define Islam. Muslims living in the West particularly feel the responsibility to take the initiative to speak out against radicalism and in favor of Islamic values of peace, tolerance, and commitment to justice. Muslim scholars have been producing works in English and European languages for decades, generally for academic audiences. But since September 11, the acute need for discourse among everyday believers has become apparent, and particularly in the United States, victim of the September 11 attacks. At countless interfaith gatherings in communities throughout the country, Muslims have attempted to present their faith to Americans whose only exposure to Islam has been the kind that makes headlines.

Typical of these efforts is a collection recently published by concerned Muslims: *Taking Back Islam*.[42] The collection includes essays by Muslims from all walks of life who felt they simply could not allow the "moral nihilism" of terrorism to be associated with Islam. Michael Wolfe explains the rationale for publishing the book: "We knew something had to be done or our religion risked being tarnished, even corrupted." He cites the frustration American Muslims feel when "anti-American fanatics quote the Quran to justify mass murder, and . . . anti-Muslim bigots quote it back – both sides using bad translations and phrases out of context . . . [W]e have sought to replace them with a truer interpretation: that Islam is a peaceful, progressive, inherently forgiving and compassionate religion. Anyone who believes otherwise misses the core values of Islam."[43]

The great play of Islamic history outlined above – from the formative period, through the medieval flowering of Islamic culture, decline, colonization, and recovery – is fascinating in its drama and breathtaking in scope. But it scarcely reflects the enduring faith of Muslims in everyday life. Many Muslims, in fact, bristle at the claim that Islam is in a period of recovery or reform. For them, essential Islam has always endured, regardless of the vagaries of history. It has endured as a daily, lived experience of faith in God's power, benevolence, compassion, and mercy. With that faith, Muslims face the struggles of daily life. The effect of centuries of political conflict and the impression of spectacular criminal acts will no doubt take time to fade. But the effort of devout Muslims to reflect their faith in daily life continues, guided by revelation – summarized eloquently in the popular Quranic verse cited above:

It is not a matter of piety that you turn your faces to the East or West [in prayer]. Righteous is the one who believes in God and the Last Day, the angels and Scripture and the prophets; gives wealth, however cherished, to relatives and orphans, the needy and travelers and beggars, and for freeing slaves; and prays and gives zakat. And [the righteous] fulfill promises when they make them, and are patient in misfortune, hardship and trouble. These are the ones who are proven truthful and are pious. (2:177)

Plate 6   The Mosque of Shaykh Lutfallah (1603–19) in Isfahan. © Peter Fraenkel.

Notes

Chapter 1

1 Scholars of Quranic exegesis (*tafsir*) study the circumstances of revelation in order to determine the applicability of verses such as these. There are several approaches to determining appropriate applications of Quranic verses. The majority of traditional *mufassirun* (scholars of *tafsir*) believe that later verses abrogate earlier verses, so that the verse revealed in Medina, after the Hijra, becomes the standard and therefore Muslims must retaliate when they have been evicted from their homes, rather than suffer in patience, as they were told to do in Mecca. Therefore, the circumstances of revelation, in this view, are especially important for dating verses. Some scholars, however, believe that applicability of Quranic verses depends on the circumstances, so that if Muslims are weak and outnumbered, as they were in Mecca, they should not attempt to retaliate, but if they are strong and able, as they were in Medina, retaliation against attacks is required. The circumstances of revelation in this view are important in order to determine such specific circumstances.

2 It is important to recognize that the term jihad does not mean fighting (*qital*) or war (*harb*). It is a generic term for struggle or effort. When military effort is required in order to stop aggression,

it is sanctioned but only when it is carried out according to carefully codified regulations that preclude surprise attacks, attacks on non-combatants, destruction of natural resources, etc. For a history of the development of notions of military jihad, and the distinction between jihad and terrorism, see Rudolph Peters, *Jihad in Classical and Modern Islam* (Princeton: Markus Wiener, 1996); and Sherman A. Jackson, "Domestic Terrorism in the Islamic Legal Tradition," *The Muslim World*, 91(Fall 2001), pp.293–310.

3   W. Montgomery Watt, *Muhammad at Medina* (Oxford: Clarendon Press, 1956), pp.221–25.

4   The term "religion" was not used in its present meaning until the modern era, when nation states replaced empires, and citizenship (being a citizen) replaced subjection to (being a subject of) the dominant power structure. In the pre-modern era, the beliefs, rituals, and hierarchies of what we call religion were deeply integrated into, and virtually indistinguishable from, the overall cultural environment.

5   This argument is developed by Mohamed Talbi, "Religious Liberty," in *Liberal Islam: A Sourcebook*, ed. Charles Kurzman (New York, Oxford, 1998), p.162.

Chapter 2

1   See al-Baladhuri, *Futuh al-Buldan*, ed. DeGoeje (Leyden: E. J. Brill, 1866) and translated by Phillip K. Hitti as *The Origins of the Islamic State* (New York: Columbia University Press, 1916), pp.110–12; Daniel C. Dennet, Jr., *Conversion and the Poll Tax* (Cambridge, MA: Harvard University Press, 1950), p.12ff; C. Cahen, "Djizya," *Encyclopedia of Islam*, 2nd edn, 2, p.559; H. Lammens, *Etudes sur le regne du Calife Omaiyade Mo'awia Ier* (Beyrouth: Imprimeire Catholique, 1930), p.226.

2   See N. J. Coulson, *A History of Islamic Law* (Edinburgh: The University Press, 1964), ch. 2–3, upon which this account is based.

3   Fazlur Rahman, *Islam and Modernity: Transformation of an Intellectual Tradition* (Chicago: The University of Chicago Press, 1982), p.32.

4   Coulson, p.37.

5   For a discussion of this claim, see Wael B. Hallaq, "Was al-Shafii the Master Architect of Islamic Jurisprudence?" *International Journal of Middle East Studies*, 25/4 (November 1993), pp.587–605.

6   "He who holds what the Muslim community holds shall be regarded as following the community, and he who holds differently shall be regarded as opposing the community he was ordered to follow." Tr. Majid Khadduri, *Islamic Jurisprudence: Shafii's Risala* (Baltimore: The Johns Hopkins Press, 1961), p.287.

7   Translated by Bernard Lewis in *Politics and War*, vol. 1 of *Islam* (New York, Hagerstown, San Francisco, London: Harper Torchbooks, 1974), pp.171–9.

8   Dennis Overbye, "How Islam Won, and Lost, the Lead in Science," *New York Times* (October 30, 2001).

9   Philip K. Hitti, *History of the Arabs* (New York: St. Martins, 1970), p.363.

10 Cited by E. B. Fryde, "History," *The New Encyclopedia Britannica* (Chicago, etc.: Encyclopedia Britannica, Inc., 1991), XX, p.566.

11 See, for example, Ronald Reagan, *Public Papers of the Presidents of the United States: 1981* (Washington, DC: United States Government Printing Office, 1982), pp.745, 871.

12 See Franz Rosenthal, tr., *Ibn Khaldun: The Muaqddimah, An Introduction to History*, ed. and abridged by N. J. Dawood (Princeton, NJ: Princeton University Press, 1974), pp.11, 13, 23.

13 See Charles Upton, *Doorkeeper of the Heart: Versions of Rabi'a* (Putney, VT: Threshold Books, 1988), pp.23, 27, 43.

14 John Moyne and Coleman Barks, *Open Secret: Versions of Rumi* (Putney, VT: Threshold Books, 1984), pp.77, 82.

Chapter 3

1   See his "Dialogues between a Christian and a Saracen," in *Migne Patrologiae Graecae*, vol. XCIV (Paris, 1860), col. 1585; vol. XCVI (1864), cols. 1335–48.

2   Cited by Philip K. Hitti, *Islam and the West* (Princeton, NJ: D. Van Nostrand Company, Inc., 1962), p.51.

3   See Terry Jones and Alan Ereira, *Crusades* (London: Penguin Group and BBC Worldwide Ltd, 1996), p.13.

4   See Jones and Ereira, *Crusades*, 52.

5   Francesco Gabrieli, *Arab Historians of the Crusades* (Berkeley and Los Angeles: University of California, 1984), p.11.

6   Cited by Gabrieli, p.12.

7 Gabrieli, pp.93–145.
8 Ross E. Dunn, *The Adventures of Ibn Battuta: A Muslim Traveler of the 14th Century* (Berkeley: University of California, 1989), pp.174–6.
9 Mohammad Khatami, *Islam, Liberty and Development* (Binghamton, NY: Institute of Global Cultural Studies, 1998), p.73.
10 See Monisha Mukundan, *Akbar and Birbal: Tales of Humour* (New Delhi: Rupa & Co., 1994), pp.7–11.
11 Quoted by Marilyn R. Waldman, "Islamic World," *The New Encyclopaedia Britannica*, 22 (Chicago: Encyclopaedia Britannica, Inc., 1991), p.127. Nasroddin had counterparts in other parts of the Muslim world, as well. He is known as Juha in the Arabic-speaking world, Nasreddin Hoca in Turkey, and Musfiqi in Tajikistan, for example.
12 Gabrieli, p.11.
13 Ibn Khaldun, *The Muqaddimah: An Introduction to History*. Tr. Franz Rosenthal (Princeton, NJ: Princeton University, 1974), pp.238–40.
14 He calls them "stupid" and "weak-minded." See *The Muqaddimah*, p.258.

Chapter 4

1 For a discussion of the various agreements between the Arabs and the Europeans, see Don Peretz, *The Middle East Today* (New York: Praeger, 1983), pp.101–59.
2 See George Antonius, *The Arab Awakening* (New York: Capricorn Books, 1965), pp.266–7.
3 See Janet Abu-Lughod, "The Demographic War for Palestine," *The Link*, 19/5 (December 1986), pp.1–14.
4 Ruhollah Khomeini, *Islam and Revolution*, tr. Hamid Algar (Berkeley, CA: Mizan Press, 1981), p.182.
5 See Alasdair Drysdale and Gerald H. Blake, *The Middle East and North Africa: A Political Geography* (New York: Oxford University Press, 1985), p.320ff, for a full description of how Middle Eastern countries lost control of their resources.
6 For the entire text of the "Constitution of Medina," reportedly dictated by Muhammad, see W. Montgomery Watt, *Islamic Political Thought: The Basic Concepts* (Edinburgh: University Press, 1968), pp.130–4.

7   Joseph Schacht, *An Introduction to Islamic Law* (Oxford: Clarendon Press, 1982), pp.70–1.

8   Translated by Fazlur Rahman, *Islam* (Chicago and London: University of Chicago, 1979), p.112, from Ibn Taymiyya, *Al-Ihtijaj bi'l-Qadar*, in his *Rasa'il* (Cairo, 1323 AH), II, pp.96–7.

9   Muhammad 'Abduh, *The Theology of Unity*, tr. Ishaq Musa'ad and Kenneth Cragg (London: Allen & Unwin, 1966), pp.39–40.

10 Nikki R. Keddie, *An Islamic Response to Imperialism: Political and Religious Writings of Sayyid Jamal ad-Din "al-Afghani"* (Berkeley: University of California Press, 1983), 103–7.

11 'Abduh, *The Theology of Unity*, pp.39–40.

12 Muhammad Iqbal, *The Reconstruction of Religious Thought in Islam* (Lahore: Institute of Islamic Culture, 1986), pp.118–21, 141.

Chapter 5

1   Nikki R. Keddie, *An Islamic Response to Imperialism: Politial and Religious Writings of Sayyid Jamal ad-Din "al-Afghani"* (Berkeley: University of California Press, 1983), p.102.

2   See Fazlur Rahman, *Islam and Modernity*, p.64.

3   See discussion by Leila Ahmed, *Women and Gender in Islam* (New Haven, CT: Yale University Press, 1992), pp.156–7.

4   See S. M. Zafar, "Constitutional Development," *Pakistan: Founders' Aspirations and Today's Realities*, ed. Hafeez Malik (Oxford: Oxford University Press, 2001), p.30.

5   Cited by Hafeez Malik, "An Introduction," *Pakistan: Founders' Aspirations and Today's Realities*, pp.5–6.

6   Shibzada Masul-ul-Hassan Khan Sabri, *The Constitution of Pakistan, 1973* (Lahore: Publishers Emporium, 1994), pp.24–5.

7   Fazlur Rahman, *Islam and Modernity* (Chicago: University of Chicago Press, 1982), pp.37–8.

8   Vali Nasr describes this process in his book about the Jamaat-i Islami, *The Vanguard of the Islamic Revolution* (New York: Oxford University Press, 1994).

9   See Abu'l Ala Mawdudi, *Islamic Law and Constitution*, ed. and tr. Khurshid Ahmad (Lahore: Islamic Publications, 1967), pp.172, 158.

10 Sahibzada Masud-ul-Hassan Khan Sabri, *The Constitution of Pakistan, 1973 (With All Amendments Up to 1994)* (Lahore: Publishers Emporium, 1994), pp.423–9.

11 Daoud Yaqub, "Deoband Gathering," April 10, 2001, <dyaqub@afghanistanfoundation.org>

12 See Akbar S. Ahmed, "Pakistan's Blasphemy Law: Words Fail Me," *Washington Post* (May 19, 2002), B1. It should be noted that no death sentence resulting from the Blasphemy Law has been carried out judicially, but there have been a number of extra-judicial killings of people accused of insulting Islam.

13 Quoted by Richard P. Mitchell, *The Society of the Muslim Brothers* (Princeton University, Ph.D. dissertation, 1960), p.524.

14 Mitchell, p.379.

15 Mitchell, p.373.

16 Mitchell, p.384.

17 Quoted by Y. Y. Haddad, "Sayyid Qutb: Ideologue of Islamic Revival," in *Voices of Islamic Resurgence*, ed. J. L. Esposito (New York: Oxford University Press, 1983), p.73.

18 Sayyid Qutb, *Milestones* (Indianapolis, IN: American Trust Publications, 1990), pp.137–8.

19 Haddad, p.70.

20 Syed Qutb Shaheed, *Islam, the True Religion*, tr. Rafi Ahmad Fidai (Karachi: International Islamic Publishers, 1981), p.3.

21 Haddad, 79.

22 See Rudolph Peters, *Jihad in Classical and Modern Islam* (Princeton, NJ: Markus Wiener Publishers, 1996), pp.107–8.

23 Abu'l Ala Mawdudi, *Islamic Law and Constitution*, p.53.

24 Quoted by Michael M. J. Fischer, "Imam Khomeini: Four Levels of Understanding," in *Voices of Resurgent Islam*, ed. J. L. Esposito (New York: Oxford University Press, 1983), p.154, from *Zendigi-Nameh Imam Khomeini* (Teheran: Fifteenth of Khordad Publishers, n.d.), II, pp.38–43.

25 Imam Khomeini, *Islam and Revolution: Writings and Declarations of Imam Khomeini*, tr. and annotated by H. Algar (London: KPI, 1985), p.187.

26 Imam Khomeini, *Islam and Revolution*, pp.210–11.

27 Haddad, p.71.

28 Sayyid Qutb Shaheed, *This Religion of Islam* (*hadha 'd-din*) (Kuwait: International Islamic Federation of Student Organizations, 1988), pp.49–64.

29 Sayyid Qutb, *Fi'l-Ta'rikh: Fikrah wa Minhaj* (Beirut: Dar al-Shuruq, 1974), pp.18–19, 310–11; Michael Yousef, *Revolt Against Modernity: Muslim Zealots and the West* (Leiden: E. J. Brill, 1985), p.177.

30 Statement by H. E. Seyyed Mohammad Khatami, President of the Islamic Republic of Iran and Chairman of the Eighth Session of the Islamic Summit Conference, Tehran, December 9, 1997, <http://www.undp.org/missions/iran/new.html>

31 Mohammad Khatami, *Islam, Liberty and Development*, p.3.

32 Khatami, *Islam, Liberty and Development*, p.11.

33 Khatami, *Islam, Liberty and Development*, pp.54–5.

34 Khatami, *Hope and Challenge: The Iranian President Speaks* (Binghamton, NY: Institute of Global Cultural Studies, Binghamton University, 1997), pp.77–8.

35 Source: *www.gooya.com*. Quoted in *Washington Post* (December 8, 2002).

36 Elaine Sciolino, "Daughter of Iran Revolution Struggles Against the Veil," *The New York Times* (April 2, 2003), A6.

37 Kamran Khan, "Gunmen Kill 7 Christians at Karachi Charity," *Washington Post* (September 26, 2002).

38 Sherman A. Jackson, "Domestic Terrorism in the Islamic Legal Tradition," *The Muslim World*, 91(Fall 2001), pp.293–310.

39 "Muslims Accept Falwell Apology," *Washington Post* (October 15, 2002).

40 "Excerpts of Bin Laden's Alleged Statement," *Washington Post* (December 15, 2002).

41 *Washington Post* (October 15, 2002), A16.

42 Michael Wolfe (ed.), *Taking Back Islam: American Muslims Reclaim their Faith* (Emmaus, PA: Rodale Press, 2002).

43 Wolfe, *Taking Back Islam*, p.xi.

Further Reading

Art and Architecture

Blair, Sheila and Bloom, Jonathan, *The Art and Architecture of Islam, 1250–1800*, New Haven, CT: Yale University Press, 1994.

Fathy, Hassan, *Architecture for the Poor: An Experiment in Rural Egypt*, Chicago: The University of Chicago Press, 1976.

Current Affairs

Ahmed, Akbar, *Islam under Siege: Living Dangerously in a Post-Honor World*, Cambridge, UK: Polity, 2003.

Cardini, Franco, *Europe and Islam*, Tr. Caroline Beamish, Blackwell: Oxford, 1999.

Djait, Hichem, *Europe and Islam: Cultures and Modernity*, Berkeley: University of California Press, 1985.

Esposito, John L., *The Islamic Threat: Myth or Reality*? New York: Oxford University Press, 1999.

Haghayeghi, Mehrdad, *Islam and Politics in Central Asia*, New York: St. Martin's Press, 1996.

Rashid, Ahmed, *Taliban: Militant Islam, Oil and Fundamentalism in Central Asia*, Waterville, ME: Thorndike Press, 2002.

Smith, Jane I., *Islam in America*, New York: Columbia University Press, 1999.

Voll, John O., *Islam: Continuity and Change in the Modern World*, 2nd edn, Syracuse: Syracuse University Press, 1994.

History

Armstrong, Karen, *Islam: A Short History*, New York: Modern Library, 2002.

Esposito, John L. (ed.), *The Oxford History of Islam*, New York: Oxford University Press, 1999.

Hitti, Philip K., *History of the Arabs: From the Earliest Times to the Present*, New York: Palgrave Macmillan, 2002.

Hourani, Albert H., *A History of the Arab Peoples*, Cambridge, MA: Belknap Press of Harvard University Press, 2002.

Jenkins, Everett, *The Muslim Diaspora: A Comprehensive Reference to the Spread of Islam in Asia, Africa, Europe and the Americas*, Jefferson, NC: McFarland, 1999.

Robinson, Francis, *Cambridge Illustrated History of the Islamic World*, New York: Cambridge University Press, 1996.

Literature

Burton, Sir Richard Francis, *The Arabian Nights: Tales from a Thousand and One Nights*, New York: Modern Library, 2001.

Gibran, Kahlil, *The Eye of the Prophet*, Berkeley, CA: Frog, 1995.

Khayyam, Omar, *Rubaiyat of Omar Khayyam*, Broomall, PA: Chelsea House Publishers, 2003.

Reference

Belt, Don, *World of Islam*, Washington, DC: National Geographic, 2001.

Esposito, John L. (ed.), *The Oxford Dictionary of Islam*, New York: Oxford University Press, 2003.

Esposito, John L. (ed.), *The Oxford Encyclopedia of the Modern Islamic World*, New York: Oxford University Press, 1995.

Glasse, Cyril, *The Concise Encyclopedia of Islam*, San Francisco: Harper & Row, 1989.

Religion

al-Quran, A contemporary translation by Ahmed Ali, Princeton, NJ: Princeton University Press, 2001.

Armstrong, Karen, *Muhammad: A Biography of the Prophet*, San Francisco: Harper San Francisco, 1992.

Nasr, Seyyed Hossein (ed.), *Islamic Spirituality: Foundations*, New York: Crossroad, 1987.

Neusner, Jacob and Sonn, Tamara, *Comparing Religions through Law: Judaism and Islam*, London: Routledge, 1999.

Sachedina, Abdulaziz and Montville, Joseph, *The Islamic Roots of Democratic Pluralism*, New York: Oxford University Press, 2001.

Rahman, Fazlur, *Major Themes of the Quran*, Minneapolis, MN: Bibliotheca Islamica, 1980.

Schimmel, Annemarie, *Mystical Dimensions of Islam*, Chapel Hill, NC: The University of North Carolina Press, 1975.

Wolfe, Michael (ed.), *One Thousand Roads to Mecca: Ten Centuries of Travelers Writing about the Muslim Pilgrimage*, New York: Grove Press, 1997.

Philosophy

Fakhry, Majid, *A History of Islamic Philosophy*, New York: Columbia University Press, 1970.

Science

Nasr, Seyyed Hossein, *Islamic Science: An Illustrated Study*, World of Islam Festival Publishing Company, 1976.

Women

Ahmed, Leila, *Women and Gender in Islam: Historical Roots of a Modern Debate*, New Haven, CT: Yale University Press, 1992.

Stowasser, Barbara Freyer, *Women in the Quran, Traditions and Interpretation*, New York: Oxford University Press, 1994.

Websites

About Islam and Muslims, http://www.unn.ac.uk/societies/islamic
The Arab-American Online Community Center,
   http://www.cafearabica.com
Islam and the Global Muslim Community, http://www.islam.org
The Muslim Student Association of the US and Canada,
   http://www.msa-natl.org
The World of Islam @ nationalgeographic.com,
   http://magma.nationalgeographic.com/ngm/data/2002/01/01/
   html/ft_20020101.5.html

Index